UNDENIABLE
God

Kim, it was a blessing meeting you. Keep in touch!

Katherine Llop

KATHERINE LLOP

FIRST EDITION

ISBN: 978-1-946466-18-1

Library of Congress Control Number: 2017942172

Published by

P.O. Box 2839, Apopka, FL 32704

Printed in the United States of America

Introduction

Everyone has a story. I am not writing this book because I think my life is different from most or because I think I am special in some way. I am writing this book and sharing my story because my story is not really about me. It is about God. This story shows a girl who fell and failed many times, and there was a God of many chances who was there to pick her up every time. This story is about a girl on a journey called "life" on this earth.

This life has been full of good times and bad times, troubles and blessings, and even supernatural occurrences. Life is a journey. We are only here for a little while. On this journey, we will all be seeking, searching for answers. We will all be reaching for something to make us feel whole in this life. We will search for the meaning of life and why we are here. We will look all over the place and, most of the time, in all of the wrong places. Many will find the surface, temporary answers to all of these. Some, however, will find the truth.

Everyone has a story. This is mine.

CHAPTER 1

Normal

I am amazed at how far back the brain is able to remember. I remember the house I lived in until I was three years old. I can walk through the entire house in my head. My mother was an amazing homemaker. She had impeccable taste in furnishings and decorations. Our living room had two wingback chairs with doilies on the armrests and a marble lamp sitting on a table between them. I specifically remember these because of the warm memories I have of spending time in my mother and father's laps in those chairs. I would climb into my father's lap when company would visit. My mother would hold me close and answer all of the child-like questions I had. I loved sitting in the arms of my parents who made me feel safe and secure as a child.

Whenever I sat with my father, I would lean out just a little away from his face. I couldn't stand the feeling of his itchy beard as he rubbed it on my cheek. At night when he would tuck me in and give me a kiss, he would purposely rub his "barba" on me. "Barba" is what my father called his beard, or any facial hair, for that matter. He would pin me down and rub my cheek and say, "Barba! Barba!"—knowing it drove me crazy! "Stop!" I would laugh and scream, loving every minute of it.

My mother was the typical wife and mother. She took care of the home, the cooking, and the children. There was consistency in our meal times, bath times, and bed times. We were always groomed and well dressed. My mother took extra pride in dressing me, as I was the only girl. Frilly socks and dresses and bows in my hair—this is how I looked in every picture as a young child. My mother—from my socks to my pajamas, carefully selected every piece of clothing. My mother's pride in these kinds of things made me feel loved. These might sound like simple things, but they were the kind of things that made me feel loved and cared for. My mother's actions spoke the words, "I am paying attention to you. I care about you." It's amazing what children pick up on early in life. Parents' actions speak loudly—positively or negatively—to the hearts of their children.

As a child, I loved to play with baby dolls. I had one doll that never left my sight. She was my attachment object, or "lovey," as some call it. She was a gift to me when I was a year old. I gave her a name right away. My mother said that I looked at her and said, "Numina." Numina went with me everywhere. I couldn't sleep without her and if she was nowhere to be found, panic struck the household. My mother had to retrieve her late one night from a store where I left her. One time, she dug Numina up from the back yard where my older brother, Joseph, buried her. She was basically a part of the family.

I learned later on in life is that "numina" is actually a word. Numina is the plural form of the Latin word "numen," which means "divinity" or "divine presence." Coincidence? Obviously, the doll was not alive or divine. However, as silly as this might sound, sometimes I can't help but think that this was a prophetic utterance as a child…or was it a coincidence? Call it what you want; I will just leave it at that. It is no secret that the presence of God has been constant in my life. He has always been with me and He wanted to make sure I knew it.

My family moved when I was three years old. At the time, my family included my mother, father, two older brothers and, of course, myself. My brother, Scott, was the oldest and my brother, Joseph, was the middle child. We moved further out from Atlanta towards the suburbs. The neighborhood we moved to was filled with young families like ours so we had plenty of playmates.

Most days you would find me playing outside. If I wasn't tagging along with my brothers, I was in the cul-de-sac or back yard with my friends. I was a bossy kid and I admit it. If I had friends over, I always took the lead and told everyone what to do. I would conduct school lessons in my room, whether I had real friends or only dolls that lined up on the floor. I would write on my chalkboard and read stories to the "class." Outside, I would march my friends around and tell them what we were going to play. I was a natural-born leader and all of the kids listened to me.

My desire to lead everyone around me didn't stop at home. At the preschool I attended, I had a group that followed me around the playground. One day I lead my friends in a song called *This is the Day*. "This is the day! This is the day that the Lord has made, that the Lord has made! Let us rejoice! Let us rejoice and be glad in it, and be glad in it!" We sang our little hearts out that afternoon. One of the preschool teachers came up to us and asked, "Girls, will you sing that song for me again?" Three of us lined up next to each other and sang to her. She smiled as she listened. When we finished, she told us that she would love to have us sing that song at our preschool graduation.

The day of our preschool graduation was a day of celebration. We had caps and gowns, cake, and an audience of parents with flashing cameras. We marched to the front of the building and lined up in front of the crowd of families. At the beginning of the graduation ceremony, two of my friends and I sang, *This is the Day*. I remember feeling proud that I got a spotlight moment at my preschool graduation. This might give away my age, but my graduation gift from my parents was Disney's "The Little Mermaid" on VHS. This was the beginning of what seemed like a never-ending marathon of "The Little Mermaid" for my father. I made him watch it with me so many times that, to this very day, he can probably still tell you what is going to happen next and maybe even sing along a little on some of the songs.

As you can see, I was a normal kid living what most would consider a normal life. I had parents that loved me and cared for me. I had big brothers that I followed around and annoyed most of the time. I had friends and baby dolls. I loved school. I enjoyed taking long bubble baths, bedtime stories, singing, and dancing. Life was good. I felt secure. There was consistency in my life and I didn't ever expect anything different.

As a young child, you learn from your parents what family life is like, what being loved feels like, and what it feels like to be secure and protected. They teach you and show you what "normal" looks like. I, for the most part, had a "normal" foundation laid early in life. I was a happy child and being happy was normal to me.

In the first grade, I began to notice some things in my home that were not exactly *normal* any more.! There were things that caught me off guard and startled me. I would hear my parents' fight and my brothers crying. I would hear screams. I saw clothes get thrown over the balcony and into the living room. I would see my parents in each other's faces yelling. I got confused and scared.

I remember feeling scared and thinking, "This isn't *normal*! This is nuts!" My house got out of control, and it got out of control fast. There were time periods where things would settle down for a little bit, but the fighting continued and as it did, it got worse. It got worse for everyone in the house. My brothers didn't laugh as much as they used to. Instead, they cried. I don't remember crying. I remember being in total shock.

One night, as I was soaking in a bubble bath in my parents' bathroom, my mother called us together to have a family meeting (minus my father). Then she announced, "I'm pregnant. You all are going to have a little brother." Nobody responded. There were blank stares and silence. Then, Joseph broke the silence. "Are you going to put him up for adoption?" he asked. Yes, he was being serious! Joseph already had "middle child syndrome." The thought of another child coming in to this family was clearly overwhelming for him.

Not long after this announcement was made, another one was made. I was riding in the car with my mom and brothers. It was a dark outside with heavy rain. I still remember the sound of the rain against the windows and the windshield wipers on high. My mother turned the radio down. Looking straight ahead as she was driving she said, "Dad and I are getting a divorce."

Frilly socks and dresses—my normal.

CHAPTER 2

The Goodbye

Months had gone by. The family was still under the same roof. I woke up one morning to my grandmother, Nonna, standing at the bottom of the stairs in my house. "Come on, Katherine, we have to go to the hospital. Your mother is having the baby!" she said. After my brothers and I got ready, we headed to the hospital to greet our new sibling.

I didn't like what I saw when we walked into the hospital room. My mother looked like she had just been through a tornado and had to hold on to a tree for dear life. I stood back, looked at her, and forced a smile on my face. I didn't understand what just happened in there, but I knew I didn't want to get too close.

Joseph saw the time at the hospital as an opportunity to run wild and play on the elevators. Being the tagalong that I was, I followed him wherever he went. We left my Nonna without telling her where we were going. We stopped on almost every floor of the hospital, got on an elevator that we were not supposed to be on, and ran screaming through the nursery. Nonna caught up with us. "Joseph and Katherine! Get over here right now!" she said in the loudest whisper she could make. Our screams and laughter filled the nursery as we tried to get away. This was a terrible thing to do on a floor with newborn babies. I'm sure the staff was not happy. Nonna was not happy at all. We got in a lot of trouble that day.

I was seven years old when Michael was born. I was a proud big sister. When my mother came home with him, I couldn't wait to hold him. I sat down in the rocking chair in my mother's room and she gently positioned him in my arms for a picture. With a huge, proud grin on my face, she snapped a picture. I still have that picture. When I look at it, I'm reminded that this was the beginning of the end. It was just a few short months after this that my mother left.

I never saw my mother pack any of her belongings. She didn't sit me down and tell me that she was leaving. One day, she was just…gone. I continued going to school and carried on with life the best I could.

On Christmas morning, my mother came over to the house. She handed me a gift. It was a small, rectangular object. I took off the wrapping paper to find a cassette tape. The label read: "*I Will Always Love You,*" by Whitney Houston. She put the tape in a cassette player and pressed *play*. We sat in the living room and listened as the song played,

> *I hope life treats you kind*
> *And I hope you have all you've dreamed of*
> *And I wish to you, joy and happiness*
> *But above all this, I wish you love*
> *And I will always love you*

She held me and cried and told me to play this song if I ever missed her. This was the moment I realized that my mother was really gone. I finally cried. I didn't understand why my mother wanted to leave us or why I couldn't go with her. Confusion and sadness set in—deep in my heart. This was the last Christmas I spent with my mother as a child.

One afternoon, I got off the school bus and saw a moving truck in the driveway. "No!" I thought. "I don't want to leave my home!" It was the only thing left that made me feel *normal*. The only happiness left in me were the memories I held in that home.

Our next-door neighbor, who had become a good friend of the family while we lived there, offered to let me live with her for the remainder of the school year while I finished the second grade. Her name was Coretta. She was a nurse. She was a friendly lady who lived by herself. She did not have children of her own and was not married. Coretta was always very kind to me and even came over one afternoon to confirm that my nose was broken after a sledding incident. After much begging, my father agreed to let me stay with Coretta. He realized I couldn't handle any more big changes in my life. My mother leaving was hard enough.

I had been staying with Coretta for 2 weeks when suddenly late one night, my father showed up to take me to our new home in Atlanta. It caught me off guard and I got very upset. Another lady in the neighborhood—my best friend's mother—came over to try to console me. I was screaming, crying, and running around the house, trying to get away from my father. The very last sense of *normalcy* I had was about to be taken from me. I was in an utter rage. However, my father would not leave without me.

As I was forced into the car, I was put in the front seat with my Nonna, who was waiting in the car with my brothers. I kicked and screamed at the top of my lungs. I never cried so many tears as I did that night. I was so angry that I bit my father's fingers as he drove away. Nonna tried to get me to stop but my father insisted that I just *let it out*. His hands were like leather. It was amazing. He kept driving and didn't flinch one time.

By the time we arrived to our new home in Atlanta, I was exhausted. It was late at night. To my surprise, we did not pull into a neighborhood with houses. We pulled into an apartment complex—complete with a personal trash man that went by the name of "Q"! He would come by at night to ask my father if he could take our trash out for money. *Welcome to Atlanta.*

I felt like the rest of my life had been ripped apart and a sense of depression came over me. My heart was broken. I had to finish the second grade in one of the most awful elementary schools in Atlanta. I was a sad, new kid. I didn't make any friends in school. I kept to myself and didn't talk to anyone. At home, the atmosphere was not warm and loving. I don't recall my father being around much and I remember always feeling hungry. It was clear to me that my father was having a very hard time trying to make ends meet while raising four kids. There was never much food in the apartment. I didn't get tucked in at night like I used to. Nobody was around to talk to me or show me affection. It was an extremely lonely time for me.

One afternoon as I was searching for something to eat, I found a sweet potato. Desperate to eat something, I called my Nonna for directions on how to cook it. She told me to set the oven to 350 degrees and bake it in aluminum foil for one hour. An hour seemed like an eternity to me as a child. Without any other options, I followed Nonna's instructions. This was the first time I baked anything on my own. Once it was done, I cut it open and put a big chunk of butter right in the middle. A sweet potato never tasted so good. This may have been the first clue to my grandmother that we needed help.

CHAPTER 3

Nonna

Nonna to the rescue! Seriously. By the grace of God and a very loving grandmother, we moved into my Nonna's house before I started the third grade. It was quite a blessing for us, to say the least. It gave all of us a sense of stability and the feeling of *normal* again. Now my father had help with Michael, the baby. We had fresh-cooked meals every morning and night. She did homework with us, read to us, prayed with us, and tucked us in at night. She showed us affection and told us we were loved. We had a sense of *normalcy* again. These kinds of things may seem small in comparison to what most people think really matter in life. However, these things were lost along the way after the divorce. It was here, at Nonna's house, that I saw the sun shine again.

I continued to feel the abandonment and loneliness that any child would feel after a mother physically leaves, and the father is emotionally checked out. At least living at Nonna's house was a step in the right direction. While living there, God spoke to me for the first time and showed me He was real.

"Nonna" is the Italian word for grandmother. It is pronounced "no-nah." Italian culture is one of the most fascinating and rich cultures in the world. With a strong emphasis on family, faith, and food, Italians have enriched American culture and the lives of anyone fortunate enough to know them. Okay—I'm proud of my Italian heritage! I am proud of

Nonna and my Grandpapa

my big, Roman Catholic, Italian family. We know how to have fun, love others, and make lots of great food. We keep traditions alive which give us strong roots.

My Nonna was born in America, but her parents were immigrants from Italy. My grandfather, Grandpapa, came to America from Spain during the Spanish Revolution on a boat. They met, married, and multiplied. My father is the oldest of eleven children. My Grandpapa was a successful attorney in Atlanta and provided well for the family. Nonna raised the children. The house we lived in with my Nonna is the same house my father lived in with his siblings. It is an old, brick house right off the interstate in Atlanta. Countless memories have been made here for many, many people.

Family gatherings were never small affairs. It wasn't unusual for there to be anywhere between eighty and one hundred people at Nonna's house for special holidays. She always included many friends of the family and other invited guests.

These are the kinds of things that were instilled in me as a child by my family. If you are going to celebrate, invite everyone you know. Celebrate big and with your whole heart. Your family is *all* you have. Love each other. Love God. Wine is good for your heart. It's okay to be loud. People hear you better when you talk with your hands. Go to church every Sunday, and you better make it to confession!

Nonna was a devout Catholic and had plans on becoming a nun before she met my grandfather. While we lived with her, she made sure my brothers and I went to mass and CCD (Catholic Sunday school) every Sunday. She made sure we were baptized in the Catholic Church and received our First Communion. I became an altar girl, which means I helped serve on the altar with the priest during services. We carried crosses, lit candles, and rang bells.

To be honest, I dreaded going to mass every Sunday. I never understood what the priest was talking about and CCD never sparked my interest. I never read the Bible or learned about anything that was in the Bible. I just did a lot of memorizing. To be even more honest, when I started memorizing all of the prayers and going to confession, I started forming opinions about what I was asked to do. There were a few things that just didn't sit right with me.

As a 10-year-old, I remember sitting in the big, beautiful church one Sunday, thinking about all of the stuff they were throwing at me. I looked around at all of the stained glass windows, pictures, and statues. I would think to myself, "Okay, praying to saints is weird. I'm not really feeling that. The *Hail Mary* prayer is strange. I'm pretty sure I'm not going to do that anymore." I would look up and stare at the cross with Jesus on it as it hung over the altar. I thought about this Jesus guy. "Something about Jesus seems right…not going to throw him out just yet," I thought. One Saturday afternoon, Nonna told me to get ready to leave because we were going to confession. I just sat at her kitchen table and didn't get up. She told me to get ready again. I looked at her and said, "I'm not going to confession. I don't need to talk to a priest.

I can just tell God myself. Also, I'm not praying to Mary or any saints anymore." Nonna stood there for a moment, leaned in, and looked me straight in the eyes and said, "The saints are the ones that will let you in the back door of heaven when you can't get through the front!"

Really? That was the mind of a devout Catholic. I never asked my Nonna if she was serious or joking, but I think there was a little bit of both in there—probably more serious. To this day, I cannot keep a straight face when I tell that story. It's a good one. I will always remember that conversation with my Nonna.

I want to make it clear that there is nothing wrong with going to confession. However, I personally feel like it could rob you of a chance to draw near to God regarding areas in which you struggle. We are all capable of having a personal relationship with God. I do not have anything against the Catholic Church. Catholics are Christians and members of the family of God. However, I decided at a young age that

My altar girl uniform.

Catholicism wasn't "it" for me.

Life at Nonna's house was good. I loved school again and made lots of good friends. Every weekend I was at a friend's house, or they were at mine. It was the 90s and being a 90s kid rocked! We had the pleasure of enjoying 90s music (real music), TV shows such as *Saved by the Bell* and *SNICK*, trapper keepers, inflatable furniture, telephones with cords and delicious snacks every kid had to have—like Gushers and Dunkaroos.

On the outside, I was happy and enjoyed life. I found happiness where I could, but deep down I still missed my mom and wished my dad would notice me. I was very sad on the inside. I felt like a huge inconvenience in my father's life and I knew my mother didn't want me in her life. I wondered if she ever thought about me. I didn't feel loved by either of them. We were all created with the desire to *love* and *be loved*. I just didn't know where to find it.

Yes, my Nonna loved us and cared for us. She gave us attention and did everything she could to give us what our parents couldn't. Unfortunately, when a parent abandons a child—either physically or emotionally—everything that tells a child they are loved is gone. The child starts to think there is something wrong with them and that it is their fault. These things cut deep into my spirit and wounds started to form.

Once wounds are formed, the door of your heart is opened to the enemy. John 10:10 says, *"The thief* [enemy] *comes only to steal and kill and destroy"* (emphasis mine). Yes, I am talking about what most people refer to as demons, devils, the enemy, Satan, the angel(s) that fell from heaven, and any other term used to describe what comes against God's creation and the will of God. I call him *the enemy*. Believe me. He exists. If you don't think he does, then he has you right where he wants you. That is exactly what he wants you to believe. If given an opportunity, he will come right on in and start whispering lies into your heart. He continuously said to me, "Nobody loves you. You're not worthy. Your own mother left you! How could anyone else love you? You're nothing.

Nothing good will come to you in life. Your life is meaningless. You might as well be dead." Since children are innocent and vulnerable, the enemy can start attacking them at a young age.

Nonna did everything she could to give me a normal life. She threw me a birthday party when I turned 10 years old. She invited all of my friends, had a cake and a piñata, and even took us swimming. This was the only childhood birthday party I had after the divorce.

Life went on at Nonna's. Elementary school came to an end and it was time for our fifth grade graduation. I was particularly excited about this since we were having a cap and gown ceremony on our last day of school and our families were invited to come. I saw this as an opportunity to grab my father's attention. Maybe I could even make him proud.

I brought the information home to my father about graduation. I thought for sure it was something he would want attend. Considering how well I did in school and my high scores on the standardized tests, I thought he would be proud to be at my graduation. When he told me he would be there, I remember the relief that came over me! I just wanted my father to recognize me and pay attention to me—something I didn't feel like he had done in a very long time.

Graduation day arrived. Everyone was full of excitement and the fifth grade hallway was quite noisy that day. We were done with elementary school and had an entire summer ahead of us! We put on our caps and gowns, lined up outside the cafeteria, and began our processional to the stage. As I walked on the stage, I saw parents and teachers and flashing cameras. I was grinning from ear to ear and began scanning the crowd for my father. I looked from one side of the cafeteria to the other. I looked in the front, the back, the sides, and all through the middle. I looked in the very back corners of the room and near the entrances and exits. My father was not there. My heart sunk. I felt some of the worst disappointment I've ever felt in that moment. Tears welled up in my eyes. Right before the tears streamed down my face, I saw a familiar face in the crowd. There, sitting in the middle of the room, was my Nonna, holding my little brother. Unexplainable relief came over me. I felt myself breathe again and my nerves calmed. I fought back the tears in my eyes and I perked up to walk across the stage when my name was called. My Nonna made eye contact with me and smiled and waved. God blessed me with an amazing grandmother. There is no question about that. I smiled, waved back, and graduated from the fifth grade.

Something happened inside me that day. I was already living with a broken heart— a wounded spirit. However, something else cut deep into my spirit that day. The last glimmer of hope I had that maybe—just maybe—my father cared about me was snuffed out. The thought that I was insignificant and unimportant to my father, settled deep within my spirit and became the *truth* that I believed. From that day forward, I knew that both of my parents had no interest in my life.

Summer kicked off with a lengthy sleep over with one of my best friends, Lacey. Lacey and I lived in the same neighborhood that I lived in before the divorce. She moved close to my Nonna's house and I loved having her around. I spent the summer with other friends, too. We did all of the normal things kids our age did during the summer. We played at each other's houses, went swimming, watched TV until late at night, snuck snacks out of the kitchen when everyone was sleeping, and slept in. Being a kid was glorious.

Many changes were starting to take place in my life, too. Not only had I moved up from elementary school to middle school, my friends and I were entering new stages in life. I didn't seem to be as resilient as I used to be. All of the brokenness of my heart and wounds in my spirit became harder to deal with. Thoughts that I wasn't loved or even worthy of love settled in my mind and spirit. Little by little, my behavior started to show that there was something wrong. I began telling lies here and there for no reason at all. I did things that I knew I wasn't supposed to do, simply to do it. I started to feel a yearning to find something to fill my voids. I wanted to find something to make me feel valuable and loved. I didn't know how or what to look for, but I had this feeling inside me that I needed to go out and find it myself.

CHAPTER 4

There has to be a God

Ibegan a new chapter in life in middle school. My friends and I were changing. All of a sudden, we were not little girls and little boys anymore. We were developing adolescents. Even the way we socialized and spent time together changed. Instead of staying home and having sleepovers, we were allowed go to the mall or the movies on our own. Boys were allowed to meet us, too. I was ecstatic to finally reach the age of increasing freedom.

I had a grandiose group of friends. We had a large group that started forming in elementary school and continued to grow. I lived in an area of Atlanta where there happened to be many Jewish families. Without realizing it until I was older, literally all of my friends were Jewish. I gravitated toward Jewish friends my entire life. I became very familiar with what Friday night Shabbat dinner was like and what kind of foods they had to stay away from during Passover. Understanding how strikingly similar Jews and Italians are has helped me realize this may have been a good reason why I gravitated towards them my entire life. I also found out later that my maiden name is a Sephardic Jewish surname. I suppose we gravitated toward each other because of our kindred spirit!

Back to the similarities of Jews and Italian, first off, Jews and Italians look a lot alike. They just do. Both cultures talk with their hands.

Both cultures love food—lots of food. They're loud. They're loving. They like to dance. They're honest—too honest. Leave it to a Jewish or Italian woman to let a skinny person know that they need to eat more, make them lots of food and sit there, watching them eat it. They never let go of tradition. Family is everything. A Jew or an Italian will dish out guilt whether you deserve it or not. So, quite frankly, I felt right at home around these people!

One particular Friday night, well into sixth grade, a large group friends and I made plans to meet at the movie theater. Nonna was always the one who drove me to friends' houses, birthday parties, or social gatherings. I was dressed and ready to go out and met Nonna in the kitchen to head out to the car. Right as I was about to leave, I told Nonna I had to run back upstairs to do one more thing. I ran up the stairs and all of a sudden, something unfolded right before my very eyes. I immediately recognized it. I was living in a moment that I had dreamed about the night before. Not one thing was different. There were certain details emphasized in my dream that I saw that moment. It was so real and so shocking that I froze. It scared me…as if I was looking at a ghost. I felt goose bumps all over me. As I stood there, I thought, "How is this happening?" It was a very intense moment.

I stood there in utter shock and blanked out for a moment—taking it all in that I was seeing what I saw the night before in my dream. It did not feel like reality for a moment. My *very* next thought was, "There has to be a God." Interesting, right? I didn't think, "I have psychic powers!" or "Wow, what a coincidence." It was too extreme and specific to be a coincidence. I knew it was not of my own "powers" or anything of that nature. All I could think was, "There really is a God! There really is a God! Oh my, God!" My gut reaction was that God had shown me something before it happened. Nothing else made sense. How could I have seen something before it happened? There had to be something beyond this natural realm. There had to be a supernatural realm. If there was a supernatural realm, then there had to be a God. It was undeniable. There was no other explanation. Human beings are not capable of seeing the future. I was amazed.

From that point forward, God began revealing things to me in dreams. I was not aware that God had been speaking to people for thousands of years, as it is recorded in the Bible, through dreams. I did not know anything about spiritual gifts. All I knew was that I saw things in dreams and they would come to pass. I knew it was God, and that is it.

One thing I didn't understand was why they sometimes seemed so insignificant. I wondered why God would give me a dream about something someone was eating and the next day I would be sitting with that person, looking at the exact same plate of food that I saw in my dream. Why? Shouldn't a message in a dream concerning future events be a little more important than what someone was going to eat? It was insignificant things like this that I would dream about, and then see it come to pass the next day or two.

I can tell you, however, that I always felt like God was saying "hello" or simply giving me a "nod" when these things would happen. It was as if He wanted to assure me that He was with me—that He was talking to me—and that is exactly how it made me feel. In those moments I was reminded that there was a God and He wasn't too busy to drop by to say "hello."

As I was changing, my social life changed and my attention began to draw away from my close friends. I began to notice people that looked like they had something to say. They stood out in a crowd and I sense what they were trying to express to the world. People with dyed hair, mohawks, chain wallets, and piercings really grabbed my attention. It seemed to me that they were intentionally flipping off the world by the way they looked. I thought to myself, "Hey, I kind of feel like that!" My wounds in my spirit had festered into deep feelings of anger and resentment. I went from a sad little girl to an angry adolescent. I was mad that my mother could just walk out on my siblings and me. I was mad that my father made me feel like a huge inconvenience and that I wasn't worth his time or affection. I was hurt. Hurt is always what lies beneath anger. I had been holding my hurt inside for a long time and it was time to let it out.

I had a teacher that year—Ms. Keeton—who had the class journal every morning. I always enjoyed writing and used this journal as one way to slowly start letting things out. I was honest, too. For some reason, I didn't mind her reading about what was going on in my life. I wrote about my family, my feelings, and the new people I was letting in to my life. The things I wrote about made it clear that I wasn't going down the right path. Yet, I needed to express myself and let things out. Deep down, I wanted someone to know.

As I journeyed into the world of expression, I found all kinds of ways to do it. I found music to be a great way to help. I listened to dark, angry, punk rock music. It was all about what was wrong with the world, the government, religion, not conforming to society, and not being controlled. I found music that expressed rage against society, family, and even God. I went from wearing girly clothing to band t-shirts and steel toe boots. The first time I dyed my hair, it was a Kool Aid red—literally. I walked around with my middle finger in the air as if to say, "Hello, world! Can you hear me? Look at me! Don't I look rebellious?"

I started running with the wrong crowd and smoking cigarettes. I drank my first beer and was rather pleased that it made me feel relaxed and happy. My problems were numbed. I didn't have a care in the world and everything was okay for that moment. Temporary joy? Perfect! Where can I get another? I didn't care what anyone thought at this point. I was mad and the world needed to know it. I was hurt and I needed to numb it.

Another year in school wrapped up. I had an entire summer ahead of me to find ways to rebel and get in trouble. At this point, I hadn't been caught in any major offenses. The only thing that was obvious to anyone was that I was being a little rebellious with my choice of clothing and hairstyles.

I was also at a point where I felt deep voids in my life. I wanted to begin a search to fill them. I didn't know what I needed. I didn't know what to look for. All I knew was that I was missing something and I needed to go find it.

At the beginning of summer break, my friend, Lacey, came to spend the night with me. I had plans for us that night. I snuck a few cigarettes out of my dad's pack and took note of where any alcohol was in the house. Once everyone was in bed, I went to the kitchen and took a full bottle of chilled white wine out of the refrigerator. Lacey and I went into the bathroom and split the entire bottle. We started giggling and came out of the bathroom. We stumbled and laughed and lost our balance. I snuck through the dining room and found a bottle of liquor. Lacey and I went into the bathroom and each took a sip out of the bottle. "Ugh! Gross! Oh my gosh! That is disgusting!" we cried as we made bitter faces and quickly put the cap back on the bottle. We returned the bottle to the dining room and retreated to my bedroom.

Laughing and singing songs on the radio, we carried on. "Let's sneak out!" I said. "Where?" Lacey asked. "I don't know. We'll find somewhere to go. Let's just go!" I answered. We put on our shoes, grabbed the cigarettes, and headed out the door. I lit a cigarette and handed it to Lacey as we walked down the road. She tried it, coughed and said, "Gross! You can have that!" We walked along the road, stumbling and laughing without a care in the world. We had no destination. We were just two girls walking along the side of the road late at night—in Atlanta. It was a five o'clock evening news report waiting to happen. The alcohol blocked reality. There is no such thing as danger when you are filled with alcohol.

As we made it to the end of the road I lived on, we saw a car coming. It passed us and we thought nothing of it. Then I noticed something odd. The car began to slow down. The driver put the car in reverse. It came to a stop when it reached us. The driver's side window came down and a male in his late teens or early twenties asked if we were okay. I grabbed Lacey's hand and ran towards the car. I opened the back door and we got in. "Take us to Little Five Points!" I said as I laughed with excitement. I had assumed this person had stopped to give us a ride somewhere! Little Five Points is a funky, alternative spot in Atlanta. You would find all kinds of people there—from street kids to hippies, thugs and punks. It was a happening place for everyone. I wanted to see where the night would take us and was ready for adventure!

"How old are you?" the driver asked as he drove away. "We're fourteen!" I yelled. "No we're not! We're only twelve!" Lacey replied. "Don't listen to her. We're fourteen! Take us to Little Five Points!" I said. The driver didn't say anything else and just kept driving. We pulled into the parking lot of a pizza place. The driver told us he needed to run inside really quick and we could get out if we wanted to. The pizza place was empty because it had closed for the night. We followed him into the restaurant. Lacey sat in a chair by the front door and I wondered around the place. Intoxicated and obnoxious, I began yelling for the driver. "Hello? Are you done? Let's go!" I wondered around the place for a few minutes. Then, I heard bells on the front door of the restaurant ring as the door swung wide open. I looked to see who could be coming in. My heart dropped. In walked a big, tall police officer. Lacey, sitting right next to the door, looked up at him with her mouth hanging open said, "Uh-oh..." I stood there in disbelief. Instantly, the fun was over.

The officer told both of us to come to the front of the restaurant and he began questioning us. He asked, "How much have you girls had to drink? What is your name? How old are you? When is your birthday? What is your parents' name and number?" Neither one of us gave straight answers. We were in bad shape. The officer became frustrated and walked both of us to the back of his car. He opened the door and told us to sit in the back. "Are we going to jail?" Lacey asked. "Yes, you are minors under the influence of alcohol. I have to take you somewhere safe until we can get in touch with your parents. If you feel like you are going to get sick, let me know so that I can let you out of the car," he replied. He stood on the sidewalk talking with the man that drove us to the pizza place. Within minutes of him closing the door, we both vomited in the back of the car. I felt sicker than I ever had. Lacey did too. Seeing how sick we were, the officer drove us to the nearest hospital to see if we needed our stomachs pumped.

A doctor evaluated both of us and, thankfully, we didn't need any kind of medical attention. We returned to the police car to be taken to the juvenile detention center. Both of us were charged with "minor in possession by consumption." We were in trouble. We were held there until our parents could be reached. It wasn't until the next morning that our parents came to get us. When I was escorted to the front of the building to be released to go home, I was surprised to see my father standing there. I was expecting Nonna, to be quite honest. He had a look of disappointment on his face as he shook his head. I got in his car and was silent the entire ride home.

When we arrived at Nonna's house, I went straight upstairs to my room. I was ashamed and embarrassed. I knew my Nonna would be mad at me. All I wanted to do was go to sleep. I was exhausted. As I lay down on my bed, the bedroom door opened. "Come downstairs, Katherine. You have chores to do and you're grounded for the rest of the summer," she said. "Unbelievable," I thought. "Nonna, I'm so tired. I can't do anything right now. Please let me go to sleep," I moaned. "Come downstairs and get the broom!" Nonna said. My summer was over.

CHAPTER 5

Little Five Points

After the summer of "no summer at all," my father decided to move us out of my grandmother's house. I didn't understand why we needed to go. Nobody else did either. I wasn't happy about it. My father already didn't pay any attention to me so moving into a new place without my grandmother would only make things worse for me. She was the one paying attention to me and caring for me. I didn't want to feel a deeper sense of loneliness. I didn't want to leave what had become *normal* to me again. My older brother, Joseph, was never fun to be around. He was mean to me and it was going to be just the two of us moving with my father. My oldest brother had moved to Florida, and my youngest brother was staying with Nonna. Once again, I was losing a sense of *normalcy*. What had become comfortable and *normal* was being taken away.

I was a different girl now. I dressed like a punk, talked like a punk, and ran around with punks. I had an entirely different group of friends—many of which did not go to my school. I remember the first day of seventh grade was a bit nerve-racking. I knew I was going to receive stares walking down the halls. I was expecting my old group of friends to ask where I had been and why I dressed so different. As much as I wanted to make a statement, I still felt a little uncomfortable. I was searching for a way to express myself. I was searching for who I really was. What was showing on the outside was not truly who was on the inside.

As I walked down the halls with cut jeans, a band t-shirt, and a pair of Dr. Martin boots, I noticed that nobody was going out of their way to approach me to ask where I had been. I kept a straight face and looked at the floor. To be honest, I didn't like walking through the halls alone. I didn't like not having anyone to talk to. It wasn't really me. I wasn't sure who I was becoming. However, I made this choice and I had to own it. So I did. I made the choice to take a path of trying to discover a "new me" and find answers.

Since I no longer felt comfortable at school, I decided one morning that I would go out to catch the bus and not get on. I waited for my dad to leave the apartment and I went right back in behind him. Skipping school was way too easy. I would spend the day smoking cigarettes and wondering around Sandy Springs, the area of Atlanta that I lived in. I would walk up to a popular hangout spot, Fellini's Pizza, and sit there for a while. I would go home and listen to music in my bedroom. Eventually, I found friends that would skip school with me.

So that it didn't become too obvious, I would ride the bus to school some mornings and leave after I was counted for during attendance. I would hop on the city transportation system, MARTA, and venture to Little Five Points. I enjoyed being down there. The people were interesting. I started making friends down there so it became my go-to spot.

The street kids down there especially intrigued me. These were people mostly in their teens and twenties that were referred to as "squatters." They lived on the streets and traveled from city to city. "Where do you sleep?" I asked a girl that had long dread locks, and clothes that were so dirty, they were permanently brown. "We find abandoned buildings to stay in. We have been staying in "the bricks" down the road for a few months," she replied. I watched the street kids "spange" every day to get money. They would sit along the sidewalk or outside a business and ask people as they walked by, "Do you have any spare change?" This was called "spanging." The street kids (or squatters) seemed like they enjoyed this life. They didn't have anyone to answer to. They stayed together and seemed very tight. They were free to do what they wanted and had a roof over their head every night. It wasn't a nice roof over their head and they were hungry most of the time, but nobody seemed unhappy to be where they were. I never heard anyone complain.

In an odd way, this lifestyle struck me as attractive—people that are with you all the time, care about you, stick to your side, and get to travel whenever they want. Life at home was lonely and this seemed rather exciting. They definitely made me feel like a friend whenever I saw them. Sometimes I didn't want to leave them.

I began making new friends all over Atlanta, but in the same crowd. Many of the people in the "punk scene" were spread out but knew each other. Joseph, my brother, was well known throughout Atlanta and was also in this scene. I tried to be my brother's tagalong, like old times, but that didn't last long. Apparently, I was still annoying to him and every time he saw me he would get on to me and tell me to go home. I began avoiding him because he cramped my style. Big brothers are so inconvenient sometimes.

As I made friends that were much older than me, I began to find places to stay and hang out for a while. These were places I could go to when I skipped school or snuck out at night. I eventually stopped going home when I was supposed to. Well, I say, "supposed to" but I would really just make an appearance at home so my father didn't call the police and report me as missing. I started "running away" for short periods of time. I didn't want to go home anymore. I felt wanted and accepted by my new friends and I wanted someone to love me. I didn't get what I needed at home and I remained so empty. I had gotten to a point where I was going to go fill that empty void myself—finding what I was missing.

Since I was on probation for the "minor in possession by consumption" episode, I violated probation when I wouldn't go to school and ran away from home. My father reported all of it to my probation officer. I had to appear before a judge in the juvenile courts for "unruly behavior." My probation officer suggested that I be incarcerated for 2 weeks while I waited to appear in court since I was a "runaway risk." The probation officer told me that boot camp would be recommended. Boot camp was a program that offenders could be enrolled in for 30 days to a year, or even longer.

When I was brought to the juvenile detention center, I was filled with fear and began to cry. The feeling of being locked up in a place that you cannot get out of is one of the worst feelings in the world. You can't eat when you want, sleep when you want, watch TV, talk on the phone, or go outside. My father came to visit me during those two weeks. He brought me a Snickers candy bar and a Coca-Cola (since I *am* an Atlantan—the home of Coca-Cola). As he sat at the visiting table with me and I ate my Snickers, I glanced up at him and I saw him wipe away tears from his eyes. I was confused. "Why is my dad crying?" I thought. "Since when did he care about me?"

I spent every day in that detention center begging God to let me go home. I lay curled in my bed all day and night, soaking my pillow with tears, saying, "Oh God, please don't let me get sent to boot camp. Please let me go home." After two weeks, I was transported to the courthouse to appear before the judge. I walked into the courtroom. I stood before a beautiful woman with a kind face and demeanor. Her name was Judge Hatchett. You may have seen her daytime show, *Judge Hatchett*, or her appearance on CNN—but this was before she became famous.

A few statements were made about me and who I was, and that I was there for violating conditions of probation by being unruly, running away from home, and truancy. The recommendation was made for me to be sent to boot camp for 30-60 days. I stood there shaking and holding back tears. My father stood at a microphone, ready to speak to the judge. The judge looked at me and looked at my father. She looked down at the paper in front of her. She crossed her arms and looked up. "Katherine, I'm not going to send you to boot camp. You don't need boot camp. I am going to order that you and your father attend counseling. You just need some help. You're going to be okay. I want you to attend counseling and start talking to someone. Don't run away from home. I don't want to see you in this court room again," she said.

Thank you, God! Thank you, God! I get to go home! I couldn't believe what I was hearing. This woman was so nice! She wasn't even the judge I was supposed to be in front of that day. As I listened to her, she looked me in my eyes and spoke to me from the heart. I could feel it. I could tell with every word that came out of her mouth that she genuinely did not want to see me in a courtroom again. I was extremely grateful that day.

I went home and I complied—for a little while. My father found a counselor for me to start seeing individually. The first session was, well, awkward to say the least. A woman took me into a padded room with a pillow and sat down with me. "Go ahead, hit the pillow," she said. "What?" I said. "It's okay. You can hit the pillow, hit the wall with the pillow, and scream. Do whatever you want. Just let it out. It's safe here to let out all of your anger," she said. I gave her a blank stare. I shook my head "no" and folded my arms. "This place is weird," I thought. I did not feel like beating up a pillow and screaming. When I got in the car, my father asked how it went. I told him never to bring me there again.

My father made an attempt to have "date nights" on Wednesday nights with me. We went to my favorite place—Fellini's Pizza. We would sit down with our slices of pizza and he would try to make small talk with me. I didn't even know how to talk to him and honestly, I didn't want to at this point. I was so hurt, so wounded. All I could feel all the time was pain. I didn't care about going to eat pizza on Wednesdays. It didn't tell me my mom or dad loved me. It didn't tell me I was worthy to be loved. It didn't tell me I deserved a good life. It didn't tell me I was worth anything to anyone. I was too overcome with feeling worthless and unlovable. I believed a lot of lies about myself at this point in life. Nobody cared about me—especially my parents. My brother hated me. If my own family didn't love me, nobody else would. My life didn't matter. What's the point in even living? These were the thoughts I woke up with everyday and went to bed thinking.

One day, I went to school and left in the middle of the day, as I had many times before. I hopped on the train that took me to Little Five Points. I met up with the street kids I had gotten to know over the past couple of months. That day, I decided I wasn't going home. I decided I would stay with them. I asked them when they would be heading for a new city. None of them knew, but assured me it would be soon. I had made up my mind. I was going to leave Atlanta and all the pain behind. I would travel to a new city with a new "family" and begin a new life. I wanted a new life. I couldn't take the pain of my reality anymore.

"So, where are we going to sleep tonight?" I asked one of them that went by the street name "Kranky." *Everyone* went by a street name. Kranky, Sparky, Space Boy, and Gonzo are some examples of the names of people I ran around with. Seriously. Kranky was a lost soul with a green Mohawk and a terrible addiction to heroine. "Come on, I'll show you. It's down Moreland. Everyone calls it "the bricks." He and a few others lead me on a journey down Moreland Avenue to an old, abandoned apartment building—"the bricks." The grass was grown up all over the property and the windows were boarded up. I thought, "Cool. So this is the life of a street kid." It didn't bother me one bit. Before we stepped foot on the property, they all took a look around to make sure no cops were around. "Don't ever let a cop see you coming or going from this building. It's against the law and they'll take you to jail," one of them said.

We ran across the front of the property and to the back of a building that faced the road. They led me to a door that would take us to the side of the building that "belonged" to this particular group of squatters. There was a long, wooden board in the place of stairs that led to the door. We walked up, went in the door, and they showed me the spaces filled with mattresses and candles. There were blankets, pillows, and people's personal belongings. Nobody had much. Anything anyone owned fit into a backpack. Traveling from city to city by hopping on trains made it hard to bring anything but some clothes with you.

"This is it!" one of the girls said to me. Her name was Kim. She was only a year or two older than me and we became very close during my stay on the streets. Interestingly enough, we even had the same hair cut. Before I made my journey to Little Five Points to become a "squatter," I shaved my head and left long bangs in the front. I dyed the bangs purple. This haircut was called a "Chelsea." My father almost fainted when he saw me the first time after I did this, but I didn't care. I had taken "flipping off" the world to a new level that day.

The people I hung with instructed me to only come back to the building after dark when I was ready to go to sleep. Nobody was to be there during the day so not to attract attention. There were other people that stayed in other buildings—runaways, drug addicts, fugitives, and homeless people of all kinds. However, if you ever did anything to attract attention to the building or got caught by police while coming or going, you were not allowed to go back. At night, you could only burn one candle in one room. You were to whisper if you were talking to anyone and had to lay low if you heard the screeching brakes of the Atlanta City Police cars. They patrolled the area every night and would ride by, spotlighting "the bricks" to see if they saw anyone. They never searched the property unless they had a reason to. As long as you laid low, were quiet, and were careful not to attract attention in any way, you were allowed to stay.

One night, when I was not there, the Atlanta police raided the place and loaded a number of people into a "paddy wagon," or police van, and took them all to jail for trespassing. They knew people trespassed there all the time. Every night we took a risk sleeping there.

The first night I stayed in "the bricks," I was overwhelmed with emotions. I was excited in a way because I had never been on my own. I was nervous because I didn't know what to expect. I didn't know the people I was sleeping under the same roof with very well. All I had that night was my book bag and a mattress to lie on. As I lay there in silence, I thought to myself, "Is someone out here going to love me?" My thoughts trailed off to my mother. I wondered where she was and if she was thinking about me. I felt the confusion stir in my head. I felt my chest begin to tighten and sadness and anger rose up in me. "Why doesn't she want me to be with her anymore?" Tears rolled down my cheeks. My last thought before I fell asleep that night was, "I want my mom."

Most mornings, everyone would leave at the same time. This lowered the possibility of attracting attention if people came out of the building at different times during the day. If you were still asleep when everyone else was ready to leave, they would wake you up. We would walk to Little Five Points to hang out on the corners or grassy areas. Most of the day was spent "spanging" and just hanging out with locals. Sometimes, we would go to people's houses for a little while to drink or smoke pot. Every evening, a pizza place would give us leftovers and that would be our dinner. Everyone knew what days food trucks would come to hand out food or what soup kitchens would be open. We would get food that way, too.

During this time, I experimented with many different drugs. I already knew how alcohol made me feel—free of worry or pain, relaxed and happy. I smoked marijuana pretty often. This was something everyone seemed to do and it was all over the place. There were three effects of this drug—hungry, happy and sleepy. Again, this was another escape from reality. I also tried cocaine. Cocaine became my drug of choice, if I were to have a drug of choice at that time. I didn't have the money to support a regular habit, however, the "up" feeling that it gave me was what I liked the most. It would speed me up, and in that accelerated speed, I felt like I could take on the world. Nothing could stand in my way. The other drug I became familiar with while I was on the streets was LSD, or acid.

The first time I ever tried LSD was on a Saturday night in Little Five Points. One of the street kids, Sparky, had an entire vile of liquid LSD. As we were walking to Little Five Points from a house we visited earlier, he stopped to take the vile out of his backpack. We were standing on a bridge over a major highway in Atlanta. Cars were buzzing below us on the highway and right by us on the bridge. It was the beginning of a Saturday evening in the city. He opened it, tipped his head back, and dropped one drop onto his tongue. "You want a hit?" he asked. "What is it?" I replied. He looked surprised and with a smile said, "It's acid." I stuck my tongue out and he dropped one drop on my tongue. "That's probably all you'll need since this is your first time," he warned.

By the time we reached Little Five Points, the ground was moving beneath me. I could feel the sounds coming out of his mouth when he spoke. His face changed every time I looked at him and we were laughing uncontrollably. The stars in the sky were magnified. The sound of the cars on the road felt like sound waves entering my ears in a fluid, non-stop motion. It was like one long "zoom" sound of cars passing by me. I looked at my hands and it looked like my own skin was crawling around. Everything was brighter and louder in Little Five Points than usual. Every light seemed to be extremely bright and every sound magnified. I could hear every conversation going on around me and I felt like everyone was looking at me.

Out of nowhere, a street poet approached me and started reciting poetry to me. I looked at him with my eyes wide open. All of a sudden, his face turned green and his long hair turned into moving snakes all over his head. The poem he was reciting was an original piece he had written about a girl that was lost and found dead in the streets. "Whoa! Stop!" I said to him. He smiled at me and his smile curled into his cheeks. "Stop! I don't want to hear anymore!" I yelled. I ran to find Sparky. He realized the "trip" had turned bad for me and it was time to get out of there.

Nights like this—roaming around, getting high, meeting strange people, putting myself in danger—is what it was like for me living on the streets. You might wonder how I showered or got clean clothes. The truth is, I didn't have clean clothes. Squatters do not wash their clothes or take showers unless someone invites them into their home to use the shower or washing machine. I was lucky enough to have become friends with a few people that lived around Little Five Points and they let me use their showers a few times. Living on the streets is dirty and smelly.

There was one person from home that I kept in touch with while I was away. She was a friend that went to school with me. She even skipped school with me a few times to visit Little Five Points during the day. Her name was Christen. Christen was a very good friend. She was honest, kind, and really cared about people. She was funny and loud— like me. We got along very well.

I would call her from time to time from pay phones and ask her to come down to Little Five Points to hang out with me. She made plans to meet up with me one night on a weekend since she couldn't during the school week. I was extremely excited to see her. That night, I had been hanging out at a friend's house that lived a few miles from Little Five Points. I asked them if I could get a ride down the road to meet her. They agreed. We pulled in and parked next to the pizza place. I was being much more careful about being seen in public, at this point, because I knew the police and my family were looking for me. I stayed in the car until I saw Christen. When I did, I jumped out, ran over to her, and greeted her with a huge hug. "Hi!" I screamed with excitement.

As I unlocked my arms from around her neck, I saw out of my peripheral vision a very familiar face. It was my Aunt Christina, my father's sister. She looked directly at me as she stood far away, trying not to be noticed. I panicked and jumped back in the car. All I could think to do was lock the doors and hope that the driver would come back and take off. She ran over to the car. "Open the door!" she yelled. I was panicking! "They've found me! They're going to turn me in to the detention center!" is all I could think. I was stuck. I had been found. I was tired. I was dirty. I was lost and didn't know where I was going.

I looked out the window and saw the concern, love, and seriousness in my Aunt Christina's eyes. "Open the door!" she yelled again. I opened the door. As soon as I did, she jumped in, almost on top of me and wrapped both arms around me tighter than I had ever felt anyone wrap their arms around me. "What are you doing?" she cried. "What are you doing?" Everything inside me broke. I let out a big wail and cried.

I got out of the car with my aunt in total surrender. Christen was standing on the sidewalk crying. She looked at me and said, "I'm sorry." She had set me up. She had been communicating with my dad the whole time. I wasn't mad at her. As I looked away from her, I saw my father standing in the distance. I ran to him and cried and wrapped my arms around him. Did I miss him? Was I glad to see him? Did I feel guilty? I wasn't sure why I ran to him. But I did. I felt his sides jump as he cried. He didn't say anything. He walked me to the car and we all got in. "You know we have to turn you in to the detention center, right?" my Aunt Christina asked. I nodded my head. I had violated probation by running away and skipping school—unruly behavior again.

We pulled away from the pizza place and drove down the road to the nearest gas station. "Do you want anything before you go? Anything to eat?" she asked. "A Snickers bar and a Coke." I said with my head down. My father got out of the car and went inside. I was so scared and so tired. I knew my probation officer was going to be waiting with a waiver to send me to boot camp. It's all I could think about.

My father came back to the car and handed me a Snickers and Coke. He called for a sheriff to meet us in the parking lot of the gas station to transport me to the juvenile detention center. When the sheriff arrived, I told my aunt and father goodbye and got into the back of the car. I breathed in my last breath of fresh air from the outside before getting in the car. There's always that last moment of freedom you keep playing in your head when you are incarcerated.

I didn't know how long it would be before I saw my father again. I didn't know if he cared. I assumed he was relieved that he didn't have to worry about me anymore, at least for a little while. As we drove through the city, I took in the last sights of free people walking around. I took in the scene of the city lights lighting the night sky. I thought about what the other street kids were probably doing while I was on my way to be locked up. I watched out the back window as we drove further away from the city.

We pulled up to a large facility with fences all around it. Barbed wire lined the top of the fences. We stopped at a sliding gate with barbed wire at the top. We waited for a few seconds. I heard a loud buzz and the gate slid to the right. We pulled through to the intake and booking door. I was let out of the car and escorted into booking. A female officer patted me down. I was ordered to take off my shoes, earrings and jacket. She opened a cell door and told me to go in and have a seat. "Dinner trays have already come around. Do you need something to eat? Breakfast trays won't come until 6:00 AM," she said in a harsh tone. "No, thank you. I'm fine." I replied.

I looked out the small, narrow window of the cell. I was smelly, tired, and melancholy. With every bit of honesty and sincerity in my heart, I looked up to the night sky, tears running down my face, and prayed, "I don't even know what to say. Just do what's best for me, God." I don't know where that prayer came from in that moment. Every time you hit rock bottom in life, the only way to look is up. And I always did.

CHAPTER 6

The Last Run

"Llop, come with me." I hopped up as I was directed by a detention center officer to come with her. She led me to a small meeting room. I walked in and sat down at a small table across my probation officer. "You ran away again. I'm recommending 90 days in boot camp. I need you to sign this waiver," she said. I picked up the pen and signed my name. I got exactly what I was expecting. I wasn't surprised, but I was very sad. I had no contact with my father or any family members for the 90 days I was in boot camp. My father didn't come to visit me or write me any letters. Nobody did. It was a long stretch of lonely incarceration. I had no idea when I would be transported to boot camp. Some people waited months to be transported. I was stuck in the juvenile detention center, waiting to be transported. It was not easy.

A few weeks later, I was transported to Pelham, Georgia to a juvenile boot camp facility. Pelham is in South Georgia where it is extra hot and humid. I was there the entire summer. I was nervous to see whom I would deal with the next few months. What were the girls like? Were any of the officers nice? Am I going to be yelled at all the time? It was nerve racking.

Immediately upon arriving at the facility, I was frisked, had a picture taken of me, given a uniform, and thrown into a line with other girls to march to the dorm that I would be living in for the next few months. We marched through the halls and into a large room filled with bunks lined up side by side. I didn't make eye contact with anyone as I walked to my bunk. I carried only personal items, such as shampoo and a toothbrush that the facility provided.

I only talked to one girl in that place for the entire three months, and I didn't talk to her often. The days went by fast as we weren't given much time to sit around. I was lonely. I didn't see my dad the entire time. I didn't get any visits or letters. I tried calling home but the phone was never answered.

There was only one person in the outside, free world that accepted my collect calls and wrote me back when I wrote him. His name was Mike. He was one of my many Jewish friends that lived down the road from my Nonna's house. I met him a year before my father moved us out. We would talk on the phone a lot, went to movies together, and chatted on America Online, one of the first social sites on the Internet. We lived close enough to walk from our houses to meet half way— just to talk and hang out. He was a good friend and an extremely good person. His friendship and contact with me during my time in boot camp meant the world to me. Not surprisingly, I recently read an article on the Internet that recognized him as one of America's most inspiring rabbis in 2015. Good people like him deserve that kind of recognition and I was happy to see that he is still a light shining in this world.

I can remember laying on my bunk at night thinking to myself, "How did I get here? What has happened to me? What is going to happen when I go home? Is my father going to come get me? Why won't he come visit me or write me? I want my mom. Where is she? Why doesn't anyone love me?" These were the same thoughts I'd always had. Nothing ever changed. It was clear that I was looking for something. I was looking for love. I found a false sense of love and acceptance, when I ran away from home, and got involved with other people that were just as lost as me. That didn't bring me anything but suffering even though it felt better to run from the pain and suppress it for a while. I was a mess—a little girl and a big mess.

After three long months of marching, eating when I was told to, going to bed when I was told to, and racing through three-minute showers, it was time for me to be released. A sheriff from Atlanta back to the juvenile detention center transported me. The following day I was released. I was ecstatic to finally go home to enjoy every day freedom— eating when I wanted to, walking to the refrigerator when I wanted to, going to bed when I wanted to, enjoying the outdoors when I felt like it, watching a little TV and taking a long shower.

I hoped my father would be happy to see me. I was hurt that I didn't see or hear from him the entire time I was gone. I was angry, but I still loved him. He was my father and I wanted him to love me. I imagined I would walk out of the detention center to be greeted by my smiling father who was excited to see me. I imagined he would walk toward me and give me a big hug and tell me he was happy I was coming home. Instead, I walked out to see my father standing there with a look of uncertainty and absolutely no excitement to see me, whatsoever. I really wanted a hug in that moment. I wanted him to be happy to be taking me home with him. I wanted so badly to feel that I was loved and missed. None of that happened.

We said hello and walked to our own side of the car to get. I didn't get a hug. Not much was said. What was supposed to be a moment of joy and excitement for me turned out to be a huge let down. I could hear deep within my spirit, "He doesn't love you! He doesn't even like you! Why would anyone miss you or even want to be around you? Your mother doesn't and, clearly, your father doesn't. You're nothing and not worthy! Nobody cares about you." I could feel it and I believed it 100 percent.

I started the eighth grade a couple of weeks after returning home. I had yet to receive one hug from my father, or anyone, for that matter. I returned to school feeling out of place and, in general, uninterested in life. I began skipping classes again. I visited Little Five Points. Many of the street kids I stayed with were gone. Only some remained. I reunited with old friends. After a couple of months being home, I decided that there was still nothing for me at home. I decided that if I wasn't going to be loved at home, then I would leave again. At this point, I stopped thinking clearly and didn't care about consequences of my actions. As far as I was concerned, there was nothing worth living for. Who cared anyway? The only thing that shut the voices out of my head was running away to numb the pain. It was insanity. True insanity. I did the same thing over and over, expecting a different result.

But, what is a person supposed to do? We are all created in the image of a loving God and designed for love. I was stripped of everything that told me I *was* loved. I was driven to do anything to fill that void. I was so empty. I yearned for the very thing I was created for—love. It drove me to do crazy things.

After I turned 14, I packed my bag again. I had a change of clothes, some money, a brush, deodorant, and a hoodie to keep me warm. I left the apartment one last time. It would be the very last time I was in that apartment. I went straight to Little Five Points. It was the same routine down there. However, I was adamant about finding a way out of Georgia. I had to leave this time. I had to get far away. I couldn't go back to jail and I couldn't go back home. I asked all the squatters if anyone was heading out of Georgia soon. Nobody ever had a straight answer or a plan. I was nervous to be back in Little Five Points without a plan. I knew the police and my family would look for me within the next 24 hours. I decided to hide indoors as much as possible, hoping for a ride out of Georgia as soon as possible.

Two weeks later, I walked through the middle of Little Five Points late at night. I assumed it would be too late for anyone that knew me to be looking for me. I was starving. I hadn't had anything to eat in a couple of days so I went to see if the pizza place had any leftovers. As soon as I thought the coast was clear, in an instant, my father, Aunt Christina and a few other family members surrounded me. My heart skipped a beat. NOT AGAIN! I did not want to make a scene. I thought about taking off, running on foot, which I had done many times before. My father still tells me today, "Man! You were fast!" In this situation,

I had two options: I could run away on foot while they probably had someone waiting in a car to chase me down, making a ridiculous scene and embarrassing myself; or I could go with them and just run away again sometime later. I chose the latter. It was no big deal to go with them and leave again. I had run away from home so many times at this point. I was quite good at it.

I surrendered and got in the car with my dad. As we drove through Atlanta and towards the general area that we lived in, I realized we were not headed for my father's apartment. I began to feel nervous and asked, "Where are we going?" My father replied, "You're Aunt Olivia's." Now, filled with nervous confusion, I thought "Well, I definitely won't be getting away tonight!"

My Aunt Olivia was the third child to be born of Nonna's eleven children. She was the mother of my two cousins, Elizabeth and Stephanie. I grew up with Elizabeth and Stephanie like they were my own siblings. Aunt Olivia was someone in the family that continuously reached out to me, taking me under her wing as a child. I went on family vacations with them, was included in birthday celebrations, spent many nights in their home, and was treated like one of her daughters. Still today, Aunt Olivia acts like a mother to me. She is filled with an enormous amount of love, strength, beauty, and compassion. She is a lovely woman who cares about people, but you do not want to cross her or try any funny stuff with her. There was a fear and respect for her that I did not have for anyone else growing up. Therefore, I had no plans of trying to escape from her house that night.

We pulled up in her driveway and parked outside the garage. She met us at the door and quickly escorted me to the room I would be sleeping in for the night. I was given a pair of pajamas and told, very nonchalantly, that we were going to Boys Town in the morning. "Wait. What? Where?" I asked. There was no conversation about it. My Aunt Olivia was smart. She didn't talk or waste time giving her opinion about the situation. The light was turned off in the bedroom. She told me goodnight and that she loved me. Then, she got a pillow and blanket and set the house alarm. She closed the door and lay down on the floor, right outside the bedroom. Even though I had no plans on escaping that night, there was a 0% chance I could if I wanted to.

I lay in the bed and with immense amounts of nervousness and confusion, I thought, "Where the heck is Boys Town?"

CHAPTER 7

Boys Town

I awoke to the sound of Aunt Olivia's voice. "Come on, Katherine. It's time to get up and get dressed." Aunt Olivia always sounded like she was singing in the mornings. I have so many memories of being a young child and having sleepovers with my cousins. Aunt Olivia woke us up with something that always sounded like a song: "Gooood moooorning, giiiirls!" It was always a happy tune to wake up to.

I came out of my sleep with a jolt of nerves shooting through my body. I had no idea what the day would bring. I didn't know what to expect. "Boys Town" sounded foreign to me. I didn't know where it was or how long I would be there. I was too nervous to ask questions. Aunt Olivia brought me to her room to find some clothes to wear. "You can't wear jeans in first class. Here, put this on. I'll find you some shoes to wear with it." She said, "FIRST CLASS?" I thought. "Oh, boy. We have to *fly* there?" My heart sunk. Everything, including Aunt Olivia, was moving and happening too fast. I was rushed into a pair of her clothes, which I absolutely hated. I had on a button up blouse with women's khaki pants and a pair of her adult, black shoes. Oh my, I could have vomited. Any 14-year-old would want to vomit. Not only was I wearing women's clothes, but also I still had my purple Chelsea hairstyle. Yes, a shaved head with long purple bangs. It was a strange combination. I was mortified.

49

In Aunt Olivia's clothes with my Chelsea hairstyle,
fresh off the streets of Atlanta, heading to the airport
to fly to Boys Town.

As soon as I was dressed, we got into her car and headed to the Atlanta airport. I remember having a blank stare most of the drive, thinking, "Is this really happening?" The closer we got to the airport, the more low-flying planes I began to see. Planes were taking off and coming in. We flew in first class all the way to Boys Town.

It was October of 1998. My walk from Aunt Olivia's car to the airport entrance was the last time I was going to feel the fresh, fall air of Atlanta for a while. Fall in Atlanta is always very mild and the cool air is something the Atlantans looked forward to after a long, hot summer.

We checked in and headed to our terminal. As we approached the gate of our flight, I saw, above the check-in counter, our flight number and "Omaha, Nebraska" on a sign. "Nebraska? Where is Nebraska?" I thought. I had no clue where Nebraska was on the map. I didn't know if I was heading north, south, east or west. Everything was confusing. I couldn't believe I was about to board a plane with my aunt.

Our flight landed in the Midwestern state of Nebraska where everything is flat, people seem much taller, tornadoes are common, and cornfields are everywhere! Once we exited the plane, the tallest man I had ever seen in my life greeted me. He seemed like a giant. I don't know exactly how tall he was, but I'm sure 7 feet is not far from his actual height. "Hello," he said as he came forward with a big smile and a firm handshake. He informed us that he was from Boys Town and would drive us to the main campus to meet the executive director, Father Peter.

As we drove by cornfield after cornfield, I began to think to myself, "Wow, there is probably no way I could run away from this place." I scouted the land as we drove. It didn't look good for me.

Driving down the highway, I saw an exit sign above that read, "West Dodge Road—Boys Town." I had to take a deep breath. We exited the highway and came to the entrance of what looked like a college campus, of sorts. At the entrance of the Boys Town campus, there was a statue in the middle of the two driving lanes that was made of resin. It was a statue of two brothers. One boy carried another on his back. The inscription on the bottom read, "He ain't heavy Father, he's my brother." That's the Boys Town motto. It originated from the words of a Boys Town youth carrying a boy on his back that had difficulty walking because of the leg braces that he wore. The boys at Boys Town would take turns carrying him. It was also the inspiration for the song *He ain't heavy, he's my brother*, written by The Hollies in 1969.

Boys Town is a place of help, healing and hope. In 1917, a Roman Catholic priest by the name of Father Edward Flanagan, opened a home for troubled and neglected boys. Father Flanagan, 31-years-old at the time, spent his time ministering to the homeless on the streets of Omaha. He understood that children who were orphaned or in unstable environments were at high risk for delinquency and crime in later years. He opened the home to all races and religions. He started with just four boys. The home quickly filled up with children sent to him by the state and others that wondered there off the streets.

Father Flanagan did not believe there was such a thing as a bad boy. One of his famous quotes was, "There are no bad boys. There is only bad environment, bad training, bad example, bad thinking." So Father Flanagan developed a program to help boys learn about family life, build healthy relationships, use proper manners, and most importantly, develop spiritual growth. This makes them productive members of society. Boys and girls at Boys Town learn the most basic life skills. These were such concepts as the steps to accepting a decision—look at the person, say okay, do the task, and check back. Boys Town youth also focus on proper greeting skills, relationship-building skills, honesty, impulse control, and how to live without chemicals. There is a long list of target areas and skills that have been developed in the Boys Town teaching model. Each youth has a specific plan of action and certain areas of their lives that they will focus on to become the best person they can become.

Today Boys Town is a village of its own outside Omaha. It is filled with nice homes, apartments, schools, a Catholic and Protestant church, fire station, police station, hall of history, and farmland. Each youth sent to Boys Town lives in a home with a married couple and their children if they have any. They are called "Family Teachers." The youth live in a family environment. Each youth is assigned chores and take turns cooking meals during the week. All of the families attend church on Sundays. As mentioned earlier, Boys Town is open to all religions. If one needed to attend a synagogue, temple or mosque, transportation was provided to the appropriate place of worship. The campus also had a Catholic church on the grounds since a Catholic priest started it. Father Flanagan is actually buried at the Catholic Church on campus. The families go on family outings, such as going to the movies or out to dinner. During football season, there was always one thing all of the families wanted to do and that was go to the Boys Town High School football games. Boy, were they good.

We arrived on campus and were brought to meet Father Peter, the Executive Director of Boys Town during my stay there. A man with white hair, glasses, a loud voice, and a big smile greeted us. "Hello! I'm

Father Peter!" he said as he looked at my hair. I watched his eyes move from my hair to my aunt and then back to me. He didn't say anything but his face said it all—"Yep, you need to be here." From that day forward, every time Father Peter saw me he would call me by name. "Hey, Katherine! How are ya?" I was amazed that Father Peter could remember so many names. He called everyone by name and made every youth feel important. Nobody was just a number.

It was an extremely memorable moment the first time I stepped into the home where I would be living. The front door opened and as I took my first step in, I felt a wave of warmth and love come over me. It was so strong and so real that it took me by surprise. It was almost tangible. I was totally caught off guard and was not expecting that. I had never felt anything like it before in my life. There was energy in the air that I could physically feel and I immediately recognized it as "love." When I felt this wave of love hit me, it felt as if it could have knocked me back. There are some moments in life that are hard to explain. This was one of those moments. The presence of love in this house was very strong.

Many smiling faces surrounded me. Each one put their hand out to shake mine and told me their name. My first set of family teachers at Boys Town was a kind couple from Texas. Their names were Chris and Tiffany. They helped me get settled and familiar with the routine at Boys Town. They were young, funny, and energetic. They gave me a book, *Don't Sweat The Small Stuff*, as a welcome gift. I still have the book sitting in my living room.

Orientation lasted a week. I had testing and meetings with clinical specialists, Father Peter, and other staff. I toured the campus, learned the history of Boys Town, and toured the Hall of History. All Boys Town youth are required to watch the movie, *Boys Town* during orientation. *Boys Town* was a movie produced in 1938. It starred Mickey Rooney and Spencer Tracey. One of the characters, Whitey, ran away from Boys Town a couple of times, only to return and eventually give into the love and help provided by Boys Town. I, of course, identified with this character—and even lived out some of his actions. I ran away from Boys Town twice during my stay there. Once, the first day I arrived and the second time during my sophomore year. Oh, I put up the fight! It was scary to think about actually letting someone love me, even though that's all I really wanted. I didn't want to open up. I had such a wounded spirit that I built a wall and wasn't letting anyone through it. I did everything I could to guard whatever was left of my heart. I realized I didn't want to let anyone in.

After orientation was complete, I was sworn in as a citizen of Boys Town. It was official. I belonged to Boys Town and it was my home. I had a plan tailored to my needs. The areas my family teachers focused on with me were building healthy relationships, not being impulsive and living drug-free. I was able to skip the eighth grade and was placed in the ninth. I was thrilled that my first day in school would be in the high school. I could not believe I was skipping a grade!

I was very involved in high school. While living in a loving, nurturing environment far from where my problems were in Georgia, a part of the real me surfaced and I flourished. I became friends with just about every person I met. I liked everyone and they liked me! I did well in school. I made good grades. The first chance I got to try out for a sport, I did. I ran track and enjoyed being part of a team. When football season came my sophomore year, I tried out for cheerleading and made the varsity cheer squad. I joined the J.R.O.T.C. exhibition drill team and went to state competitions. J.R.O.T.C. was one of my favorite classes in high school. I also played soccer and cheered for the varsity wrestling team and basketball team. I felt like I was on top of the world! I stayed busy and (almost) felt like I knew who I was again. I even grew my hair out.

In school, I took religion classes and weekly church attendance was required. Even though I felt like I didn't get anything out of Catholic masses, I still had a prayer life from a very young age. That never changed. I always talked to God. Even as an immature child, I still knew God existed. It was easy to get caught up in this life and not think much about God, but He was always there. I knew He was. I didn't read the Bible or pay attention in church, but the eternal part of me always felt the connection to the Creator—no matter how wretched, rebellious, or dishonest I'd become.

When it came to the helping or therapeutic side of Boys Town, I drifted along and did what it took to get through each day. I didn't get honest about myself or open up much. I resisted every adult that tried to get in and form a relationship with me. Well, God always has a plan to get what He wants done. All of that began to change my junior year in high school.

CHAPTER 8

The Holy Spirit

After spending a year and a half in Boys Town, there was a brief attempt to see if I was ready to return to Atlanta and try a normal life back home. My Aunt Olivia offered me a place to stay in her home. I would enter one of the private schools in Atlanta and finish high school there. I returned to Atlanta to live with her, my Uncle Bill, and my cousins, Elizabeth and Stephanie. I assured her that I was ready. However, I was not ready. I just wanted to be back in Atlanta to have more freedom. I was placed in a private Catholic high school that most of my family attended during their high school years. Unfortunately, I did not last long in Atlanta. I found plenty of trouble to get in to. It just wasn't the right time.

One semester later, I was back in Nebraska. I moved into a new home on campus with a new set of family teachers. "The Stewarts" was the sign that hung outside their home. Their names were Mac and Kerry. Mac was an ex-cop from Illinois. He even looked like a cop. He was also extremely funny and kept everyone in the house laughing all the time. Kerry was a kind, sweet lady with piercing blue eyes and red hair. Her voice was soft and she always had a genuine smile on her face. They were people devoted to God and answered a call from God to leave their lives in Illinois to become family teachers at Boys Town. They grew up in Illinois, met in church, got married, and had two little girls. They were a lovely family and people full of love. They set a beautiful example of what marriage, family, friendship, and service to others looked like. They sacrificed every day to try to make a difference in the girls' lives in their home.

The first night I was back in Boys Town, I walked into our basketball team's home game to make my big appearance. "Kat! Kat, you're back?" people yelled from the bleachers. "Hey!" I yelled back and waved. I didn't really want to leave Atlanta, but being back at Boys Town wasn't all that bad. Everyone that waved and yelled to me from the bleachers looked happy to see me and, honestly, I was happy to see them, too. Boys Town had become my home away from home. I enjoyed being involved in school and having so many friends. I had a great set of family teachers. "I can do this." I thought to myself. "It's not so bad."

It was easy to settle back into the routine at Boys Town.

I picked up right where I left off in school. I immediately got back on the cheer squad, joined the exhibition drill team, and was asked by the J.R.O.T.C. instructor if I would command the regulation drill team.

Within my first week living with Mac and Kerry, I could feel that something was going to be very different this time. I had been floating through the system at Boys Town since I arrived there in 1998. I wasn't a problem child. I didn't do much to get into trouble. There *were* a few times I got into trouble and sometimes it wasn't small trouble. However, for the most part, I was a pretty good kid on campus. I followed the rules, which moved me up in the system, and I told everyone what they wanted to hear. The problem was that I never let anyone "in." I didn't open up any more than I had to. I resisted opening up, being honest, and building any kind of relationship with any of the adults in my life— including my family teachers.

It didn't take Mac and Kerry long to figure me out. One day, Mac asked me, "Have you ever seen *Good Will Hunting*"? "No." I replied. "I want you to see it. I think you need to see it." Mac said. After months of me living in their home, Mac and Kerry saw right through me. They saw that I would do what I was supposed to, do well in school, get involved, and do all of the other things that were expected of me. They also saw that I had walls up all around me and never really got honest or open with *anyone*. That evening, Mac rented *Good Will Hunting* and sent me up to the loft in the house to watch it alone.

The movie was about a man named Will who grew up in South Boston. He was a 20 year old, undiscovered genius with a troubled past. He worked as a janitor at M.I.T. and anonymously solved an impossible math problem posted outside a math class. After a run-in with the police and facing jail time, Will was taken under the wing of the math professor to study under him and seek therapy. Will's rude behavior and unwillingness to open up lead therapists to refuse to treat him any further. Finally, the math professor, who really wanted to help Will, made a final attempt and called in his former college roommate, who taught psychology at a community college. This psychologist challenged Will's defense mechanisms and after a few sessions, Will began to open up. Will was unable to build relationships with others and be honest with them. Suffering from child abuse, this was his defense mechanism in life. He sabotaged any chance to build relationships with people, lied, and never lived up to his full potential. The psychologist helped Will to see that he was a victim of his own inner demons and that it is not his fault. Will began to experience healing. He continued to open up and be honest. He became a changed man. He got a job, grew into his potential, and pursued a real relationship with a girl.

When the movie ended, I got the point Mac was trying to make. I definitely saw myself in this character, Will. It also struck me hard when I realized, "Oh, no. They have me figured out." Mac and Kerry saw that I was—not to brag—pretty intelligent. They saw that I was a hurt child inside who refused to be honest with others as a way of protecting myself. They saw that I would not open up and build relationships with anyone. All of my relationships were surface and somewhat artificial. They saw that I needed inner healing and they wanted to help. So, they challenged my defense mechanisms and the walls I had built up. They didn't sit me down and challenge them with psychological pieces. They simply challenged them with pure, pure love.

One night when everyone had gone to bed, Kerry and I sat on the couch carrying on light conversation. God was brought up in the conversation and Kerry began to share with me a little bit of her testimony. She talked about being raised in church and being told about asking Jesus into her heart. She said that she was a teenager when she asked Jesus to come into her heart and wasn't even 100% sure about it, but did it anyway. Being raised Catholic, I didn't hear about saying a prayer to ask Jesus into your heart. She told me the prayer she prayed. She said her life was never the same. I listened and was curious about how this whole thing worked. I, too, thought the same thing Kerry thought, "What is this about? I'm not really sure about this. Is this real? Exactly what does asking Jesus into your heart mean? I know about God, but what about this Jesus guy?"

I thought about it again when I went to bed that night. As I mentioned earlier, I've always known that God existed but never sought Him on a deeper level. However, I wondered what this whole "asking God's son into your heart" thing was all about. In an earlier chapter, I mentioned that sitting in the Catholic Church as a child, I would go through and toss out things that were taught to me that I didn't agree with. The only thing I didn't toss out just yet was that Jesus guy. I thought, "I don't really know what this is all about but if I it can help me go deeper with God, that would be pretty cool." As I lay in bed that night, at 16 years old, I said the prayer that Kerry told me she said to ask Jesus into my heart. "Jesus, I know that I'm not perfect and I know that I'm a sinner. I ask that you please come into my heart, wash me clean of my sins and live inside me." Then, I rolled over and went to sleep.

Now, I have heard many different testimonies of what happens to people after they ask Jesus in to their hearts. I will go ahead and say that nothing radical, or life changing, happened the next day. I didn't wake up to Jesus standing at the foot of my bed. I didn't start speaking in tongues or having visions. I wasn't a different person. Walking with the Lord is a never-ending process—a life-long journey. It is a continuous journey of growth down an infinite path until the day you leave this planet. We can never stop growing in the Lord. He is perfect and we are not. We can never be completely perfect or exactly like Him. We can only strive to be like Him. Just because you have decided to follow the Lord does not mean you will not mess up. I would love to say that this is where my journey with the Lord started and that my life was changed forever, but it wasn't. Deciding to walk with the Lord is a daily decision to give your life to Him and follow Him. I did not do that; it was just something new in my human experience.

Hopefully, you are wondering what *did* happen after I asked Jesus to come into my heart. Did I begin to experience God on a deeper level? Did God talk to me? Well, the answer is *yes*. Even though I did not fully understand Jesus, who He was, or what He came here for, I still had the yearning to grow near to God. If Jesus had something to do with that, it was worth a shot. As days went on, I began to notice something going on inside me that I had never experienced. It was very small, but I picked up on it and was curious where it came from. I began to feel a sense of conviction (not condemnation) from thoughts I had about the things that came out of my mouth. The voice of God is a still, small voice inside. All of a sudden I began to "hear" that something I was thinking was impure, or what I was about to say was better left unsaid. I stopped myself from letting filthy words spill from my mouth. This was just a very soft and gentle prompting from deep within. God is not loud. On the contrary, He is quite a gentleman. His still, small voice is so soft and gentle that it is actually very easy to blow off or ignore.

The conviction I began to experience is how I know for a fact that when I asked Jesus to come into my heart, I received the Spirit of God—the Holy Spirit. The Holy Spirit is the Spirit of Truth. Responding to the prompting of the Holy Spirit can make you feel really good. It did for me. If you don't respond to the voice of the Holy Spirit—which is easy to do—it will become harder and harder to hear the voice of God. Or, you can respond to that prompting and simply stop yourself.. The purpose of that sense of conviction is to keep you from going any further. If you respond to conviction, you will grow, becoming more spiritually mature. That is what we are all here for. That's the goal.

CHAPTER 9

Senior Year

Every kid at Boys Town looked forward to receiving one thing—a Senior Planning Binder. When you received this, you knew you were on your way to a cap, gown, and independence. The Senior Planning Binder was full of material to help you plan your life after leaving Boys Town. The material helped you answer questions like this: *Were you going to go to college? Where would you apply? What would you like a degree in? What scholarships and financial aid could you apply for? Would you go to Job Corps? Would you enlist in the military? Which branch? What job would you like in the military? Take the ASVAB, SAT and ACT tests. What is your GPA looking like? What can you work on to get where you want to go?* All Boys Town seniors worked on their Senior Planning Binder project throughout the year. We had regular meetings with the staff in preparation for our departure into the world. We all left with a plan.

My senior year at Boys Town High School was exciting and full of accomplishments. I was co-captain of the Varsity Cheer Squad. I was on the J.R.O.T.C. drill team and held the rank of Command Sergeant Major. I was commander of the regulation drill team and also on the exhibition drill team. I put together a curriculum for cadets' testing and review so they could move up in rank. I was the editor of the school newspaper and Senior Class Representative. I was all over the place and I enjoyed every moment of it!

J.R.O.T.C. was a class that I especially enjoyed. I liked military training, marching, learning how to properly carry a weapon, singing cadences, being involved with the drill teams, and even having uniform inspections. There was something about the military that was attractive to me. I loved our country and had a deep respect for people in the military. The J.R.O.T.C. instructors made a huge impact on me. They were both retired from the Army. The lead instructor, Colonel Jordan, was one of the kindest men I had ever met in my life and I say that with all sincerity. He was tall with gray hair and glasses. He graduated from West Point Military Academy and was a battalion commander in the war in Vietnam. You could still see shrapnel in his arms from a bomb that exploded right in front of him while he was there. He was loved and revered by many—especially me.

Colonel Jordan always made me feel like I could do anything. He put me in positions to do things that I never thought I could do. He pushed me to always do my best and put much faith in me. All throughout my life, and still to this day, God has strategically placed people in my life at a specific point in time to help me get to the next place He wanted me to be. I don't call meeting those people *coincidences*, but rather, divine appointments!

On Tuesday, September 11, 2001, I was in my J.R.O.T.C. uniform for a uniform inspection. Our school had "Caucus" every Tuesday morning in the Great Hall where all high school students would meet before class. After leaving "Caucus" on this particular Tuesday morning, I headed to my first class—J.R.O.T.C. I walked in class only to find my instructors watching the news on a TV that was in the classroom. I saw the shock on their faces. I looked on the TV screen to see the Twin Towers in New York burning. Terrorists had struck both towers in hijacked planes. Thousands of people died that day. It was a somber, quiet day on campus. Each time the bell rung to switch classes, kids filtered out of the classrooms into quiet hallways, with little to no socializing, and entered the next room where they could continue to watch the news coverage of the terrorist attacks.

From that day forward, I knew what I wanted to do when I graduated in May the following year. I had been considering a career in the military and my choice to do so was solidified that day. I had something I believed in. I believed in America and I believed in service. I was proud to live in a country where we don't have to fear daily terrorist attacks, like the one on September 11, 2001, because of good people like Colonel Jordan that served and fought to make this country what it is. My plan was not to enlist, but to enter a military college. I spent my senior year planning to enter college, major in nursing, get scholarships and other financial aid, and commission into the Army as an officer after getting my degree. My senior planning committee supported my decision. I spent the rest of the year researching military colleges, scholarships, and filling out applications.

One afternoon, Kerry told me she needed to talk to me. She pulled me aside and told me that my mother wanted to talk to me on the phone and I could call her if I wanted to. "My *mom*?" I thought. I sat numb and emotionless since I hadn't talked to my mom in a very long time. I wasn't joyful or excited. As straight as my face was in that moment, so were the feelings inside. There was not much going on inside. I was the master of suppressing emotions and putting band-aids on wounds my entire life. I lived this way everyday. Staying busy and thinking about other things masked the pain of abandonment.

I told Kerry that was fine and I would give her a call. I walked to the phone and dialed the number. I was *very* curious what this was all about. Why was she reaching out to me at seventeen years old? She left when I was seven years old and the contact throughout those ten years was few and far between. I didn't know my mother at all.

When she answered the phone, her voice was just as fresh in my mind as it was when I was seven years old. "Hi, Katherine! How are you, honey? How is school?" she asked with a cheery voice. Just hearing my mother's voice brought the same comfort I knew as a child. It was so familiar and brought back two specific feelings I once had—protection and love. My, how I missed feeling this way!

I smiled. "Hi, mom. I'm good," I replied. I proceeded to tell her all about cheerleading, the drill team, being the Senior Class Representative, and the editor of the newspaper. I talked about my Senior Planning Binder and that I was applying to colleges that year.

It was easy to see that despite a broken spirit, I had a lot of good things going on in my life. Turning away from my old life and channeling all that energy towards positive things at Boys Town brought about many blessings in my life. I still had a wounded spirit, but I made a *choice* to do things differently at Boys Town.

As the conversation went on, my mother told me that she wanted to come to Omaha to see me. "I would love to come spend Thanksgiving with you. Would you mind if I came to Boys Town for Thanksgiving?" she asked. "Yes! Yes, that would be awesome!" I exclaimed. My mother, who I hardly knew, was coming to spend a holiday with me for the first time in ten years.

I had many things to be thankful for that Thanksgiving. I was in a home with a couple that treated me like I was their daughter, loved me for who I was, and believed in me. Mac and Kerry are the first people in years that I allowed to love me. They challenged my defense mechanisms with pure love and as a result, some walls came down and I let that love soften my heart. I allowed myself to *feel*—a little.

My mother sat at the same Thanksgiving table as me. I couldn't believe it. As I looked at my mother, I never felt pain or anger toward her. I was basking in the joy of my mother's presence and the knowledge that my mother got on a plane to come see me. She *wanted* to see me. It was a wonderful feeling, although still a little confusing. You see, I believed for years that I wasn't worthy of my parents' love or time. I didn't try to make sense of it. I just enjoyed it. I had too much going on to analyze the situation. I just took it for what it was.

After this visit with my mom, we began talking regularly. I called her to share with her the latest news on my senior planning. My college of choice was North Georgia College and State University (now

University of North Georgia) because of their outstanding military and nursing program. When I got my letter of acceptance, I couldn't wait to pick up the phone to tell her. She shared in my excitement and told me she was proud of me. My mother invited me to come live with her for the summer after I graduated so she could help me prepare to enter North Georgia. Life was good. Sometimes I had to stop and take in that life was actually *that* good. I had come so far. Everything I wanted in life was becoming a reality. I was on top of the world!

I did well in all of my classes that year, studied hard for tests, and took my planning seriously. Like I said, my senior year was an amazing year. It went by fast and before I knew it, the year was coming to an end and senior prom was upon us. This was a very exciting time! I had a red dress, a date, and was announced as a candidate for *prom queen*!

The night of prom, Kerry had someone come in to do our hair and makeup. I checked my dress, shoes, nails, hair, and face a million times to make sure I looked picture perfect. Our dates picked us up (driven by their family teachers, of course) and we headed to the venue for dinner and dancing. After dancing and making great memories with friends, it was time for the crowing of the king and queen. The candidates lined up. I stood there nervous, next to my friends. My science teacher, Mr. Kohmetscher was the announcer. He introduced each candidate. Everyone applauded after each name was called. Then, slowly filling the crowd with anticipation, he announced, "Your 2002 Prom Queen is.........*KAT LLOP*!" I gasped and put my hands over my mouth. I couldn't believe what I had just heard! Screams and clapping came from the crowd as cameras began flashing. The next thing I knew a crown was placed on my head and a blue cape with the letters "BT" on it was fastened around my neck. I was shocked and felt honored to be recognized by my peers in such a way. It was an incredible night.

The final countdown to graduation began after that. I moved through the system at Boys Town and completed my goals there. My senior year ended with awards and recognition. I received an award from the Omaha World Herald—*Key Staff Award Excellence in*

Journalism. I was awarded three scholarships to pay for college and inducted into the National Honors Society. I was leaving with nothing but accomplishments and good memories. I had come so far.

I spent a lot of time reflecting on the time spent at Boys Town. I thought about the things that stuck out the most. I thought about the moment I first stepped into a house on campus and the tangible love I felt in the atmosphere of that home. I remembered Father Peter's smiling face when he met me for the first time and how nervous I felt the first day I arrived. I thought about all of the teams I had been a part of—cheerleading, track, soccer, and drill team. I learned so much about others and myself by being part of a team. I learned how life, in general, was actually not at all about "me" but about "us." I learned how much easier it was to just say, "okay," rather than arguing. I learned what healthy relationships looked like. Mac and Kerry showed me what it looked like to have God living in their hearts. I thought about the conversation I had with Kerry on the couch my junior year. I remembered the prayer I said before going to sleep that night and the first *check* I ever received in my spirit from God.

I reflected on the first time I ever felt joy and fulfillment in my heart when I served others at a soup kitchen. Whenever I served at Boys Town, I felt joy and knew that it was part of fulfilling a common purpose that we all have. That common purpose was to know, love and serve God by knowing, loving, and serving others. True fulfillment is in service to others.

I reflected on the friendships I developed and how important they all were to me. I relived the moment over and over in my head when I heard my name announced as the *prom queen*. I knew why I was crowned prom queen that night. It had nothing to do with being popular. I know in my heart that I was crowned prom queen because of kindness. I was kind to *everyone* in high school. I didn't care who they were. I would walk and talk with anyone. I truly liked everyone in high school. Being crowned prom queen was not about me winning a popularity contest. Or…maybe I *was* popular because I was kind. This is something I still hold on to today. I am not perfect, but I do believe in kindness and I do believe kindness can get you far in life.

As we seniors took our last exams, we packed our bags and received our caps and gowns because graduation day was upon us. It was a beautiful, sunny day in Omaha, Nebraska on May 19, 2002. The campus began to fill with out-of-town guests. Graduation day was filled with cheers and tears. My Aunt Olivia, Elizabeth, Stephanie, mother, father and, of course, Colonel Jordan were all there. I graduated with honors. Afterwards, I packed my belongings in my mother's rental car and cried with Mac and Kerry as we said our goodbyes.

As we drove off the Boys Town campus, I set my eyes on the statue of the boy holding another boy on his back with the inscription that read, "He ain't heavy Father, he's my brother."

The "He Ain't Heavy, He's My Brother" Statue at the entrance of Boys Town.

CHAPTER 10

North Georgia

Boarding a flight back to Atlanta for good was a fantastic feeling. As much as I don't like the heat or sweat, I *do* love Atlanta! It is home. I had many things to look forward to. I was starting a new chapter in life. I was entering college to pursue a career in the military as a nurse. I had many new people to meet, friends to make, and adventures to have. I was happy to be where I was. Getting to know my mother was something else I had to look forward to. It was the first time since I was seven years old that I would be living under the same roof as her.

We pulled into her neighborhood and I scoped everything out. This was where I would be spending the next few months. We took a few turns in the neighborhood and finally arrived at her house. As we pulled up the driveway, the garage door opened. We got to the top of the driveway and there, in the garage, sat a black Lexus with a big, red bow on top. I looked at my mother. She smiled and said, "Go check out your car!" *What? My car?* "AHHH!" I screamed. Excitedly, I jumped out to see it. My own car! It was the icing on the cake. This year just couldn't get any better.

I visited with family over the summer—my father, Nonna, cousins, aunts and uncles. Friends from Boys Town flew in to spend time with me. We went to Six Flags, a baseball game, boating on the lake at my dad's house, camping, and had other wild adventures. I went to North

Georgia to meet other freshman that would be entering college that year. I made a couple new friends right away and spent time with them over the summer as well.

As I spent more time with my mother, emotions from my childhood eventually surfaced. They weren't feelings of loss, anger, or resentment. Instead, they were the emotions of being a child again—literally. I felt like I was five years old again—protected and secure—and giddy inside when I heard my mother's voice. I thought about my *normal* life before both parents left, abandoning me.

However, sometimes I watched my mother and her new husband talk and thought to myself, "Where do *I* stand with my mother? She knows him better than me which probably means she likes him more than me." After such thinking, my self-esteem dropped and my heart felt sick. I questioned why I was there and why my mother brought me there?

These thoughts and emotions took me by surprise. I didn't like it at all. All of that was so long ago and so much had happened in the last decade. I had to refocus. I had to push those thoughts to the side and bury the emotions that were stirred up. I knew how to do that. I told myself there were much more important things to do and think about. I wasn't seven years old anymore; I was a rising freshman in college!

As my first day of freshman orientation got closer, the mixture of excitement and nervousness began. This was going to be very different from life at Boys Town. It was the beginning of something new. I worked hard to get accepted in college. Since I was entering the military program, I had a week of "boot camp," which was called "F.R.O.G. Week." F.R.O.G. stood for "Freshman Recruit Orientation Group." I wasn't scared to march, do pushups, get yelled at, and run at 6:00 a.m. every morning. That was the fun stuff. I was ecstatic to be a part of the R.O.T.C. (Reserved Officers Training Corps) at North Georgia College.

My mother and I got up early on my first day of F.R.O.G. Week. I packed my trunk full of my belongings and hit the road. As we neared Dahlonega, the town North Georgia was in, I could see the mountaintops stretching across the sky. These mountains look blue from a distance. That's why they are named the Blue Ridge Mountains. It is something absolutely breathtaking to see. A great sense of peace came over me. I knew I was doing exactly what I was supposed to be doing in that moment of my life. All was well, as it should be.

We pulled onto campus and pulled up to the barracks. Men and women dressed in BDU's (battle dress uniform in camouflage) stood there…waiting…expressionless. Here we go! I kissed my mother good-bye and began the weeklong freshman orientation. It was everything I expected and more. We were up before the crack of dawn every morning. We did physical training, marched, learned how to do things in military style, sang cadences, went to the Army Ranger Camp just around the corner from school, went on a road march, and even received nicknames.

Oh, yes. We had nicknames and something to *sound off* when told to do so. Having a *sound off* was how you responded to a sergeant or officer when they addressed you or if they simply said, "Llop! Sound off!" or "Llop! Roll call!" I was given the nickname "Lollipop". These guys were clever. The reason they gave me the nickname "Lollipop" was because, to them, Llop sounded like "lollipop" and it tied into the sound off I was given.

If you've ever seen the movie, *The Wizard of Oz*, then you definitely remember the munchkins in Munchkin Land singing, "We represent the lollipop guild, the lollipop guild, the lollipop guild." They would kick each leg out one at a time while they sang this song. This was my sound off. I am short, like a munchkin, and had a last name that you could easily turn into "lollipop." I had to be ready in any given moment if someone yelled "Llop! Roll call!" I would stand up and sing, while kicking my legs from side to side, "We represent the lollipop guild, the lollipop guild, the lollipop guild." And they would just laugh and laugh, and so would I. Everyone was given a ridiculous nickname and ridiculous things to sound off. It was a great week full of laughs, new challenges, sweat, tears, and straight up fear. I finished F.R.O.G. week strong with Alpha Company and began my freshman year in the nursing detachment.

As many freshmen do their first year in college, my friends and I found the parties to go to. College isn't college without parties. It was a new experience and fun—and against some major rules for freshman in the Corps. As a cadet, I was not allowed to be outside the barracks after a certain time at night and I certainly wasn't allowed to be out of uniform. We were not allowed to fraternize with upper-classmen—people of higher ranks. Parties were a big "no-no" for the freshmen. So, of course, someone reported us and it was not taken lightly. The instructor interrogated each of us by recording us while we answered his questions. Then we got "smoked" by our squad leaders. Getting "smoked" is a form of punishment in the Army, which involves some form of serious physical activity. You feel "smoked" when you get done. We had to run, do lots and lots of pushups, and hold ourselves in the "ready" position, which is holding you in the pushup position for a long period time. The physical activity you were made to do when getting "smoked" is beyond physical training—it is punishment. Along with that, we were "grounded" to the barracks for two weeks and only allowed to leave for classes and PT.

My mother and stepfather were notified about the incident and the disciplinary action that was taken. My mother didn't seem too upset about it when I talked to her on the phone. She understood that I was under disciplinary action at the school and we left it at that. My mother wasn't surprised. Who goes to college and doesn't go to a party?

One morning, I woke up and walked out to the parking lot and did not see my car anywhere. I began to panic. I immediately called my mom and she informed me that my car had been taken away. "Brian and I drove up there to get it," she said in a monotone voice.

In a situation like this, if a kid responded with anger, it would show they were angry about being punished, rather than being sorry for breaking the rules. All punishment is uncomfortable and nobody ever likes consequences.

However, I interpreted this situation differently. I questioned my mother's motives and thought she put her husband's idea before what was best for me. In my mind, I was an hour from home, living on a college campus, and had no way to get anywhere. In my mind, my mother was more concerned with this husband of hers than she was with me. I was immediately filled with rage.

Old feelings of being less than important to my mother started filling my head and heart again. The band-aid I put on my heart was lifting. I let my mind run loose, the same way I did back into my childhood. Resentment came back as I thought about my mother getting remarried and never wanting to see her children. The rage came to the surface and I channeled that negative energy toward my mother. An old, infected wound was exposed. All of a sudden, my mother was not the woman I flew home with when I left Boys Town. I didn't see the mother who I loved and longed to be with since childhood. Looking through the childhood "glasses" I had on my entire life, all I saw was a selfish person who left her children to suffer on their own and chase after her own happiness.

All of the lies the enemy whispered into my spirit from childhood came up again from the depths of my heart. They were always there, but now I heard them loud and clear again. The enemy was standing right in my face, ready to take me down again with the same lies I heard as a child. "You're unimportant. You're an inconvenience. You're unlovable and unworthy of love." These lies were alive as they had ever been. All of a sudden, I went right back in a very familiar place.

All it took was one event to bring so many things to the surface and expose the old wounds in my spirit. The event itself wasn't serious at all! It's not like I was abused, mistreated, or neglected in some way. But it was the event of loosing my car that helped expose the wounded spirit that had always been there. I still had a wounded spirit that had been covered up for a long time. It took a very small thing to send me spiraling downward again. Just like a house that wasn't built on a strong foundation, I had no foundation at all!

I may have soared through high school and accomplished many

wonderful things, but I was not a strong person on the inside and the enemy was not going to stop coming after me. He waited for the perfect opportunity to take me down. I was an easy target. He knew it wouldn't take much to agitate those wounds. I believe he saw the calling of God on my life from the time I was a child. He wasn't going to stop attacking until I came all the way down.

My first year in college did not end the way I had imagined it would. I skipped classes, drank, went to parties, and took my focus off building a good life for myself. Instead, I went looking for ways to fill the voids in my heart and patch my wounds. I lived one moment to the next; never thinking about consequences and completely took my focus off my future. I didn't consider the consequences of my actions. I didn't care anymore. Sound familiar? My state of mind had changed so drastically that I didn't even feel like myself anymore. Everything I thought I had learned was now far from my memory. Every band-aid I had successfully and strategically placed over all of my wounds had lost their adhesive. They were gone.

I decided to stay in Dahlonega over the summer. I moved into a place with a girl that was also a student at North Georgia. As I slipped further and further down the wrong path, I began smoking marijuana. I would smoke all day, every day. My roommate and I loved to wake up, drink Cuban coffee, and smoke together. We would talk about life and how "beautiful" it was. Marijuana made me feel that way—peaceful and that everything was good and beautiful. It was an obvious drug of choice for someone like me who did not see myself as good and worthy.

If I didn't have to work, I would get in my car some mornings, play some music, and drive through the mountains. With a smile on my face, fresh mountain air, and a little Phish on the radio, everything seemed perfect. I was happy with drinking, smoking weed, and waiting tables. I felt like I didn't need anything else. I had lowered my standards and taken my focus off my future. Once again, I felt like I wasn't important, so why do anything other than what I was doing. I had no real purpose. When the time came to register for the next year's classes, I decided not to. I would just work and be a hippie.

I found out quickly that everyone at my job smoked weed. We would go into the back cooler and smoke before the place opened or during a break. The first time I brought my own marijuana to smoke with everyone, it was a huge hit. We went to the back cooler and I packed a pipe. As the pipe got passed around, one by one they looked at me surprised, impressed, and in awe. "Where did you get this weed?" they asked excitedly. It was definitely much better than anything any of them got and I told them I could get it for them any time. From this point on, I went to Atlanta at least twice a week to buy large amounts of marijuana. This is when I discovered that selling drugs was easy and very financially rewarding.

Life became very free. The only responsibility I had was going to work. Other than that, I spent my time smoking weed, selling it, and going to Phish shows and other jam band concerts. Phish is like today's Grateful Dead—a very popular jam band. At their concerts, you could find just about any drug you wanted. Marijuana, psychedelic mushrooms, and ecstasy were very popular at concerts. These drugs enhanced the experience of the show and I partook of all of them.

I had connections in Atlanta for all the drugs that were popular among the hippie crowd. Before I went to Atlanta, like a good salesperson, I would call around to take orders and ask who needed what. The money was fast and easy and I was good at it.

I made a lot of "friends" during this time. Many people seemed to like me—or at least liked what I could get them. I felt like people needed me, cared about me, and accepted me. However, this was far from any true love or friendship. Once again, I was searching for something, or someone, that could fill the voids in my heart. It was a temporary fix for my wounded heart that never lasted. Therefore, I constantly chased that desire to be loved.

One quiet evening, a few visitors decided to show up at my house. A guy that I had recently met and sold weed to, came over. He was a short, energetic guy with a bald head and tattoos all over him.

Just minutes after coming in my house, he handed me a picture frame. "Try this!" he said. I looked down and saw a line of a white powdery substance. I thought, "Hmm, cocaine. I haven't seen this in a long time." Without even thinking twice, I took the rolled dollar bill out of his hand and snorted it. Right away I knew that it was *not* cocaine. Nothing had burned my nose and throat like that did. I threw my head back and put my hands over my face. I scrunched my nose while tears rolled down my face. "OW!" I yelled. It hurt so bad that it took my breath away.

When I finally got myself together, asked him what it was. He looked at me and said, "Dope! It's speed!" Within minutes, we were both sitting there talking a million words per minute, fidgeting, and sweating. Everything sped up and I had enough energy to walk to California that night. My mind filled with all kinds of things to talk about and I, all of a sudden, felt very, very close to him as well as the other people in my house. It was like all of us had entered a secret club and instantly became family. "Let's go to my buddy's house. He lives just down the road." We all got up to leave. My roommate wasn't entirely sure what was going on so she stayed behind.

Once we got to the house, there were people in different rooms doing different things. Everyone was very busy. Someone was spinning music, another was taking something apart, someone else was playing video games, and everyone else seemed to be sitting around talking over each other. There was *a lot* of conversation going on.

I could not believe how great I felt. I wanted to stay in that moment forever. The entire night I sat on the floor just talking to people. Everything, including myself, was going so fast that I totally lost touch with reality. I had no idea when, but my cell phone died and I realized quite a few hours had gone by. I asked someone if I could borrow a phone charger. Once my phone got charged, it began to ring. It was my roommate. I picked up and said, "Hello?" with a very scratchy voice. I heard her frightened voice on the other end say, "Kat! Where are you? I've been trying to get in touch with you for three days!"

CHAPTER 11

Meth

One day, two days, three days went by. This was now a regular cycle in my life. After that first line of meth, my life spiraled out of control. I lost my job at the restaurant. My roommate asked me to leave. I was consumed by the constant chase of looking for the next high. I made my money the illegal way. I sold drugs to support my own meth habit and made money to survive. All my belongings fit in my car. I had no stable place to live, no real job, and lived at jam band shows with drug addicts. I didn't care. Being high all of the time gave me a false sense of peace, happiness, and that I was in control.

When you delve into highly addictive drugs like meth, you begin to mix and mingle with some very different, scary people. The first meth dealer I had contact with went by the name "Scooter," which was a street name, of course. Scooter had a lot of rules when you went to his house, as did most drug dealers.

Rule number 1: show up by yourself. He did not allow more than one person to come in his home to purchase anything. This was a way of keeping undercover drug agents out. Rule number 2: you cannot come in, buy something, and then just walk out. You had to stay for a while. People coming in and out of a house rather quickly are a good sign to outsiders that drug dealing is taking place. If the police had watched his house, it would be very obvious what he was doing. Rule number 3: you had to actually do meth with him while you were there. This was another way he thought he could rule out whether or not you were working with the police to set him up. He did not think anyone that was a cop, or working with the cops, could do meth. [That is actually not true.] Rule number 4: No talking on your cell phone while at his house. Rule number 5: when leaving his house, do not turn on your car head lights until you are completely out of his driveway and on the main road. It was nerve racking to go to this guy's house. He also had surveillance cameras all around the outside of his house and would monitor everything from his TV.

The first time I went to his house, we were just introduced. I didn't buy anything from him. It was almost like an "interview" to see if I was someone he felt comfortable dealing with. Scooter was very careful about that, as you can tell. When I left, he gave me his phone number and told me to call him whenever I needed anything.

Soon after, I contacted Scooter to buy from him. It was late at night. He opened the door and led me to the surveillance room where he dealt with people. That night, he was very high and constantly looked at his monitors and peeked outside his windows. He was very friendly and talkative, which are common effects of meth. Sometimes you feel like everyone is your best friend. As he gathered what I was buying, he offered line after line of the drug. We sat talking for hours. As the hours passed, he became more paranoid. He left the room and came back with something that I hadn't seen before. It was meth, but it was very wet and pink looking with a very strong smell to it. "Do you want to try some of this?" he asked.

I put two and two together pretty fast. He is making his own meth. At that point I got very uncomfortable. It is one thing to deal with people that sell a drug—which is very unsafe. But it's totally different when the dealer manufactures the drugs themselves. That is, without a doubt, psychotic. Understand that drugs are a tool the enemy uses to steal and destroy lives! Everything about drugs is demonic and dark. When you are manufacturing drugs, it is basically being involved in sorcery.

At this point, more drugs had been put into my body at one time than ever before. Everything was moving very fast around me. Scooter would not stop looking out his windows, checking his monitors, and pacing back and forth. He kept pushing meth in my face until I couldn't do anymore. However, the only thing that comforted Scooter's paranoia was to participate in more drugs. I tried to leave but he wouldn't let me, saying he felt like someone was watching him.

I had been there for *hours* and all I wanted to do was leave. I had never seen anyone act like this before. I sat there feeling trapped as I wondered "Is this guy going to hurt me? I've been here forever. Why won't he let me leave?" I finally stood up and yelled at the top of my lungs, "Dude! I have to go!" He looked at me with complete shock on his face. "Yeah, that's right. I'm leaving. I'm seriously about to flip out!" I said. I grabbed my purse and walked toward the door. He walked with me and said, "Ho-ho-hold on! Let me check first!" He peeked out his living room window and then opened the door to let me out. I walked quickly to my car and got in. I felt like I had just escaped a very dangerous situation. I had never been so happy to walk out of a place in my life!

I backed out of his driveway and pulled on to the main road. I drove to the stop sign at the end of the road. As I came to a complete stop, something started happening to me. All of a sudden, I saw thousands of stars in front of me. Everything went completely black. I have a very vague memory of turning my car to the left. The next thing I knew, I was in the parking lot of a closed gas station. My car was running and I was parked. As I looked around, I had no idea where I was. Panic set in. I did not know what just happened, where I was, or how I got there. It was very dark. The only lights in the area came from the gas station sign and a street light at the corner of the road.

I picked up my cell phone and called a friend. "Taylor!" I said, "I have no idea where I am. I can't drive. Please come help me!" "Ok, try to explain to me where you are. What is the name of the gas station? Can you get out of your car and walk over to a street sign to tell me the name of the street?" he asked. My vision was obstructed due to the high amounts of meth in my body and whatever happened to me at the end of Scooter's road. I got out, walked right up to the street sign, and squinted to read the name. I gave Taylor the name of the road, got back in my car, and locked the doors.

As I sat there waiting for Taylor, I tried to figure out just how exactly I got to that gas station. I remembered seeing stars and everything going black, but I do not remember driving. I was in a black void until my vision cleared. I'm not even aware of how long that lasted. It could have been seconds or an hour. I leaned back in the driver's seat and felt my body shaking, my mind racing, and my heart pounding in my chest. I was so high, I actually wondered if I was ever going to come down again.

After a while, I saw Taylor pull in. A great sense of relief came over me and I jumped out of my car, ran over to him, and hugged him with gratitude! He could tell I was shaken up. As we drove away, I tried to explain to him what had happened. To this day, I do not know what happened between the street sign and the gas station. I do believe God directed me to the gas station that night. Even in my sin, God protected me. His love and mercies are more than I can understand!

For a long time, I traveled down a dark road of drug addiction. It was evil, deceiving, and painful in so many ways. When you are living in drug addiction, you are in a state of constant deception. There were times I actually thought I was having spiritual experiences and revelations from God and did not think I was separating myself from Him. There were times I would eat psychedelic mushrooms and believe that I was experiencing heightened states of consciousness. Everything around me became symbolic and I thought I was tapping into a level of consciousness that was very deep and spiritual. Sometimes, I felt so much joy that I began to cry. These were all counterfeit experiences. None of it was real. When the mushrooms wore off, I became very tired and depressed. This is exactly what the enemy does through drug use. You put substances into your body that make you think and feel a certain way for a short period of time. You want that feeling again, so you get more. It is the cycle of drug abuse. It is dark. It is demonic and you are in chains—literal spiritual chains. The enemy has you.

One cold, rainy evening in January 2004, I was driving though Gainesville, Georgia in the middle of the night. I had been "up" or awake on meth for a few days. I was cruising down a main road through the city and was just a few minutes from my destination. As I took a turn, I noticed in my rearview mirror that a Gainesville City police car was behind me, following *very* close. It was 1:30 a.m. and nothing about the situation felt right. I just knew I was about to get pulled over. I slowed down to a very slow speed to make sure I wasn't going over the speed limit. I got extremely nervous. My hands and arms were shaking on the steering wheel. Suddenly, the bright blue lights lit up behind me. I knew right away this was not going to go well. I had methamphetamine, scales, baggies, a ledger, and a marijuana pipe in the car.

I pulled over to a side street and parked the car. "Maybe he won't search my car since I have a North Georgia College and State University sticker across my back window. Maybe he'll just think I'm some college kid coming home late from a friend's house. Just keep it cool," I thought to myself. I was about 95 pounds with a sunken face, fidgety, shaky, and had pupils so big he probably could not even see my eye color.

I rolled down my window. "Ma'am, can I see your driver's license and proof of insurance?" "Yes," I replied as I fumbled through my purse. He was not rude, abrasive, or mean. He was very calm and talked to me in a respectful tone. "Do you know why I pulled you over?" was the next, obvious question he asked. "No, I don't," I said as I shook my head. "You're tag has expired," he said. "Oh! Yes! Well, actually there has been a problem getting the title from the owner and my mother has been trying to get in touch with him and I have no idea where it is and I have been waiting for my mother to call me and let me know so that I can renew the tag and actually I have been pulled over for this before and already received a few tickets. Here I'll show you. So, I'm aware of this, officer, and I promise to take care of it. I won't drive anymore until I get it taken care of." I said all this very fast and in one breath. He paused for a moment and looked at me. "I'll be right back," he said.

In just a couple of minutes, another Gainesville city police officer pulled over to where we were parked. "I'm going to jail," I thought. A female officer walked up to my window with the other officer. This is where the "good cop, bad cop" game started. "Where are you headed tonight?" she asked in a very harsh, suspecting tone. "I'm on my way back to my boyfriend's house." I answered, voice shaking. "Why are you still driving around on an expired tag when you've already been pulled over for it?" she asked. She lifted her flashlight and shone the light directly in my eyes. "Your pupils are dilated. Are you on drugs? I can't even see the color of your eyes!" she exclaimed. "No!" I answered.

She walked away from the car to talk to the other officer. "Oh man. This is really happening. I am really about to go to jail. They are going to find drugs in here and I am going to get arrested. Oh, man. This is really happening." I began to shake. Both officers walked back to my car and began asking me questions. I kept looking away from them, but they already knew. I was caught and they were easing their way into a reason to search my car and arrest me. "Do you have any drugs in your car?" the woman asked. "No," I answered. "Well, do you mind if we search your car?" I was so scatter-brained by this point and so scared that I consented to a search of my car knowing what they would find. Did that make any sense? No. Nothing makes sense when you are on drugs. I had been awake for days. I was already confused before I got pulled over. I was not in my right mind.

As I got out of my car I was told to have a seat in the back of the police car. "You're not under arrest, we're just holding you while we search your car." "Ok, whatever that means," I thought. I sat in the back of the car and watched them completely tear my car apart. "She's going through my wallet. I have a baggie in there with meth in it. She's about to find that." I thought. I watched her lift her hand in the air toward the streetlight to get a good look at what she had just pulled out of my wallet. She marched to the car and opened the door. "What is this?" she yelled. At that point, I stopped answering questions, sat back, and looked straight ahead. She closed the door and went back to my car. I watched both officers go through every inch of my car and put every piece of evidence on top of my car—baggies, scales, drug ledger, marijuana pipe. I was done. The female officer walked back to the car as she read through the drug ledger. She opened the door and asked in a harsh tone, "Are you a drug dealer?" I looked straight ahead and didn't answer. She slammed the door shut and went back to my car to continue searching.

As the male officer went through the trunk of my car, I saw him look at something in his hand and pause for a moment. I saw a glare come off a shiny, flat object in his hand when he turned to the side. He walked over to the female officer and said something to her. They both stared at it. "What are they looking at?" I wondered. The male officer walked over to the car and opened the back door. He held up a picture and asked, "Is this you?" In his hand was a picture of me. It was a picture of me at the king and queen dance, right after I had been crowned prom queen. It was a close up of my face. I had a big smile on my face. Right on the tip of the crown was a very big sparkle, which was caught in the perfect moment in the perfect lighting. My eyes filled with tears. I shook my head, yes, and looked away from the officer. "You look like a completely different person! What are you doing to yourself?" he asked. I began to cry. "What *am* I doing to myself? What have I done to my life?" I thought.

After the officers had gone though my entire car and taken everything apart, the female officer walked back to the patrol car. "Step out of the car. You're under arrest for possession of methamphetamine with intent to distribute. You have the right to remain silent. Anything you say can and will be used against you in the court of law. You have the right to an attorney. If you cannot afford an attorney, one will be appointed to you by the state." I was frisked, cuffed, and placed back in the patrol car. The male officer drove me to the Hall County Detention Center.

By this point, I had expended every bit of my energy and

experienced an enormous amount of stress and anxiety. All effects of the drugs had worn off and I started to feel heaviness and pressure in my chest. I hadn't slept in days and all I wanted to do was close my eyes. I struggled to keep my head up and my eyes open.

When I was escorted into the booking area of the jail, my arresting officer walked in and said to the booking officers, "Look at this!" They all huddled around him and stared at the picture in his hand. He brought my prom queen picture with him to show everyone. They all looked at me, and then back at the picture. Everyone started commenting. "Wow. Whoa. That's her? Oh my god," I heard coming from the huddle. As the booking process started, the officer responsible for locking up all of my personal belongings walked over to me with the picture in his hand. He had a soft look on his face and asked, "Miss Llop, you were prom queen?" "Yes." I responded. "You sure do look a lot different. The girl in this picture looks so happy and healthy. What happened to you? Why are you doing this to yourself?" he asked. I shrugged my shoulders. "Well, I hope I never see you down here again and you get off drugs. I hope you get some help. You don't belong here," he said.

As I sat in the holding cell, I began to drift in and out of sleep. It was the middle of the night and I felt like I could have slept for days. The benches were hard and the building was cold. It also smelled like Pine-Sol cleaner and cafeteria food. I was miserable!

There is a program run by the court system called "Drug Court." In this program, defendants arrested on drug charges that don't have a prior criminal record, are given an opportunity to participate in this program. It is an intense two-year program. If you complete the program, your charge will be dismissed. You are expected to be in meetings or classes almost every day, consent to random drug screenings, and waive a few rights. Once a week you have to appear in court before the judge and the rest of the Drug Court team. If you mess up, miss a class, fail a drug screen, or do not pay your fines, you can be sent to jail for a length of time determined by the judge. This program is designed for people that actually want to get clean and stop using drugs. People that *want* to change their lives will do what it takes to get through this program. The criminal justice system is well aware that people who get arrested for possession of illegal drugs are drug addicts themselves and need help. The Drug Court program was invented to help those that *want* help. Upon entering the program, the participants have to sign an adjudication of guilt. This will be used as your *guilty* plea, if you get terminated from the program, and you will be sent back to jail with all charges reinstated.

After about 24 hours in the Hall County Jail, an attorney visited me. He was a bright, happy man with red hair and glasses. He informed me that he was the attorney for the Drug Court program. He asked if I would like to be in the program and be released the next day. I could hardly think straight when I was sitting there talking to him. As much as I didn't want to be in a cell—with two other women and sleeping on a mat on the floor—all I could think about was going back to that cell to go back to sleep. I was very weak coming off meth. "If you want to be in the Drug Court program, you will appear before the judge tomorrow and be released some time tomorrow afternoon," he said.

The next day, I appeared before the Drug Court judge, Judge Girardeu. He was a kind, southern gentleman that spoke with an accent straight out of the movie *Gone With the Wind*. It is the sophisticated southern accent that I have only heard in elderly men from Georgia and I love it. Judge Girardeu started the Drug Court program in Hall County and really believed in it. He wanted to help, but he was also very firm. He really believed in me and expected me to do very well in that program.

Within two weeks, I was trying to figure out a way to do meth and flush it from my system with large amounts of water to pass a drug screen test. Not even 48 hours after I did meth, I was called in for a random drug screen. One thing the program offered was a chance to sign a piece of paper admitting you were going to fail a drug screen before you took it. This didn't mean you wouldn't get in trouble with Judge Girardeu. It just showed that you were being honest, and maybe, Judge Girardeu would be easy on you. Since meth takes at least three days to get out of your system, I knew I was going to fail my drug screen.

Was I really ready to stop using? No. I accepted the Drug Court program that was offered to me because I was told I would get out of jail the next day. Was I able to stop using? Yes. I had all of the tools and support I needed. All it took was a *choice* to stop. However, I was missing the reason to stop using drugs. I didn't have one. I hated reality. I was a sad person on the inside. Facing life wasn't appealing to me. Living life with constant feelings of unworthiness and inadequacy wasn't something I wanted to do. In my mind, getting high on drugs made me feel good and I just wanted to feel good about myself.

I appeared the following week, with the rest of the Drug Court participants, in front of Judge Girardeu. I was sure I was going to be sanctioned a day or two in jail. I was nervous and on the verge of tears. Every participant was reviewed every week. When it was my turn, it was brought to Judge Girardeu's attention that I failed a drug screen. "Katherine, do you have anything to say?" I walked up to the microphone and let out a huge spiel of how I felt disgusted with myself and can't believe I relapsed and how I will never do it again and was very sorry. The judge looked at me for a moment and said, "I'm going to give you a free pass and not send you to jail. Don't fail another drug test!" he said. My dad always told me I should have been a lawyer. I was very good with words and persuasion.

Unfortunately, I got through a couple more weeks of Drug Court and relapsed again. This time, I didn't bother to show up to the drug screen and decided I would *run* again, since I am so good at running from things in life. Since I didn't show up to any more meetings, classes, drug screens, or court, a warrant for my arrest was issued. Going AWOL from the program was a sure way to get terminated from the program and get convicted of your charge.

I carried on for months in a drug-addicted, dark world. I saw a lot of scary things. The longest I ever went without sleeping while I was on meth was nine days.

One night I was in my apartment with Ben, who I regularly used drugs with. Ben was my boyfriend throughout my drug-addicted years.

We were sitting in a room talking and as I was looking at him, I saw something out the corner of my eye. Behind where Ben was sitting was the kitchen. I could see the refrigerator…and a very tall man standing behind the refrigerator…staring at me. I kept looking at Ben and then beyond him into the kitchen. Back and forth, back and forth, my eyes kept wondering. Ben noticed and stopped talking. He looked behind himself to see what I was looking at. He turned around and immediately fixed his gaze on the refrigerator. He looked at me and then back at the refrigerator. "Do you see something?" he asked. "Yes! Do you?" I asked in a frightened tone. He nodded his head slowly with eyes wide. We both stared at the refrigerator. "Okay, tell me what you see. Because if we're seeing the same thing, I'm getting out of here…I mean, I think we really need to get out of here," he said. "No, you tell me what you see," I said. "Do you see someone standing behind the fridge?" he asked. I gasped! I could not believe what I just heard! I stood up and froze as I kept staring at the man staring at us. We both stared at him in complete silence. He saw us. We saw him. Finally, Ben nodded his head at him and said, "Hey…." Then the man nodded, lifted his arm, and pointed his finger up at an angle. In unison we said, "Oh my god!" "Did you just see him nod back at you?" I asked, not even sure if I was still alive at this point. "Yes!" he said. We looked at each other and I said in a low voice, "Dude…let's go." We stood up, walked slowly to the front door, and watched the man behind the fridge stare back at us. "He's watching us," I said. "I know," he said. We opened the door and hurried down to the car.

Ben got in the driver's seat and I got in the passenger's seat. Ben stopped and with a look of fear on his face, stared at the sidewalk in front of the building. The look on his face scared me. "Ben, let's go! What's wrong?" I asked. He could hardly get any words out of his mouth. He just kept starting at the sidewalk. I was so scared that I didn't want to look at whatever he was looking at. He looked like he was about to start crying. "Ben! What is it? You're scaring me!" I yelled. "There are firemen over there crying on the sidewalk!" he yelled. "Go!" I screamed at the top of my lungs. I couldn't take any more. Ben started the car and took off down the road. We panicked and yelled all the things you would hear people yell after seeing what they thought were—simply put—ghosts. You can call them what you want, but when you are doing drugs, you're opening doors to the spiritual realm. That's a fact. You are opening yourself up to evil. We drove two hours north that night and didn't return to the apartment for days.

About a week later, we ran into the owner of the apartment building. We were having a casual conversation and he mentioned to us that many years ago there was a terrible fire in that building and people died.

Had we opened ourselves to darkness using drugs? How did we see the same man standing behind the refrigerator? Was it a "ghost"? Or was it all hallucinations? How did Ben see firemen on a sidewalk facing the building that we had no idea had burned down years ago?

Time went on and so did my insanity on drugs, as I chased high after high, saw "shadow people," destroyed myself, and allowed the enemy to take me down. A couple of months later, I was arrested on the warrant from Drug Court, held without bond, and was supposed to be terminated from the Drug Court program.

In Aunt Olivia's clothes with my Chelsea hairstyle, fresh off the streets of Atlanta, heading to the airport to fly to Boys Town.

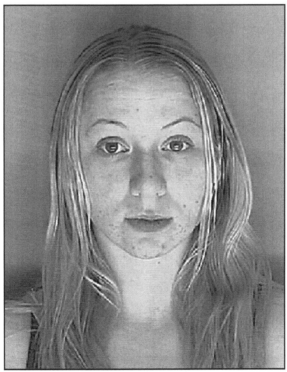

My booking photo. Addicted to meth.

CHAPTER 12

Miracle in the Courtroom

Ishuffled my way into the courtroom, shackled, to face Judge Girardeu. I sat down in the designated area for incarcerated defendants. I saw the attorney for the Drug Court program, Graham, walking quickly towards me. He sat down next to me and with urgency in his voice he said, "You know, you have the right to withdraw your guilty plea. Or they can terminate you today and sentence you to prison. That is what the district attorney wants to do. She is recommending an *8 do 4*." An *8 do 4* is an 8-year sentence, serving 4 years in prison and serving the rest of the time on probation.

Most of the time, nobody—especially a first time offender—ever serves his or her entire sentence time. They serve only a percentage of it. It's up to the parole board how much time you serve. However, nobody wants to go to prison regardless of how long you have to be there. By the way, prison and jail are two different things. I was in a county jail at this point. That is where you are taken immediately after getting arrested and where you will stay until you are bonded out, released by a judge, or transported to prison. Prison is a facility where convicted criminals are sent for a long period of time to serve their sentence.

When I heard "8 do 4," I almost passed out. I was so upset with myself. How could I have gotten myself in to so much trouble again? Why do I do this to myself? I immediately told him that I wanted to withdraw my guilty plea and get an attorney. When it was my turn to stand before Judge Girardeu, I walked up to the microphone with Graham. My hands and legs were shaking. The district attorney brought her case before him. "Defendant, Katherine Llop, charged with possession of methamphetamine with intent to distribute, has gone AWOL from the Drug Court program and has been noncompliant. I am recommending she be terminated and sentenced to 8 years with 4 to serve in prison." Judge Girargeu proceeded to officially terminate me from the Drug Court program and almost sent me to prison. In the middle of Judge Girardeu's sentence, Graham interrupted him and said, "Uh, Your Honor! Miss Llop would like to withdraw her guilty plea!" *That almost happened! He almost sent me to prison!* Usually the judge will give the defendant, or the defendant's attorney, an opportunity to say something, but Judge Girardeu went straight to the sentencing.

Judge Girardeu stopped and stared at Graham. Nobody ever withdraws his or her guilty plea when getting terminated from Drug Court. He took in a breath and looked down at his desk. He looked up and reluctantly said, "By law, I am required to let you withdraw your guilty plea. So, I will withdraw your guilty plea and this case will be set to be heard on a later date." "We would like to request a bond for her, Your Honor," Graham said. "No bond!" Judge Girardeu quickly added.

Sitting in jail with no certainty of when you will get out is a terrible feeling. However, at least I wasn't heading to prison yet. Graham talked with me once I sat back down. He said, "You'll be appointed a public defender and they should come see you within 48 hours. You could at least try to get the sentence lessened and maybe you won't have to do so much time. I don't know. It's all up to what your attorney can get the state to agree to. Good luck." There was a glimmer of hope, but I was still in a bad situation. It didn't look good for me. No court date, no bond, and terminated from Drug Court, which always resulted in going to prison!

I cried almost every day I was in there. All I could think about was fresh air, fresh food, a bed, and all the simple things that came with a free life. I was locked in a cell 22 hours a day. We were let out for one hour, twice a day—once in the morning and once in the evening. We could shower, make phone calls, and watch TV during those one hour time periods. It was very depressing and I was absolutely miserable. I spent all of my time praying. I was scared I was going to prison. I chose to believe that God didn't want that for me and I started praying like I had never prayed before.

My attorney, Mr. Parr, came to visit me. I was taken to a tiny conference room for inmates and their attorneys. He told me that he had spoken with the district attorney and they were still offering *8 do 4*. He said he would try to get it lowered. I looked at him and said, "No, I want to ask for First Offender's Act." Under the First Offender's Act, the defendant will enter a guilty plea or Nolo Contendre and upon completion of their sentence, which is usually time on probation, the judge will deem they not be convicted of the crime. This seemed to be wishful thinking. Failing the Drug Court program, signing an adjudication of *guilt* upon entering the program—which imposed an automatic sentence—and then asking for another chance on First Offender's Act is not something that had ever been done. Mr. Parr looked at me for a second and then kindly said, "I'll see what I can do. We can at least try." He smiled; we shook hands and went on our way—him back to his car in the free world and me back to my cell.

Every time I came to my senses and thought about the reality of what I had done, I would panic and cry. All I could think about was what other people went through who had been terminated from the program. They were sentenced to prison. Naturally, they were all very surprised when I told them that I got terminated from the program, but withdrew my guilty plea. "I'm going to ask for First Offender's Act." I told them. "Ha! You're joking, right? They are not going to let you out on First Offender's! You're going to prison, girl," they laughingly said. One girl even told me I should just agree to what the state offered in efforts to try to speed up my time and not sit here waiting to go to court, adding to the time I'll have to be in jail. As hard as it was to hear all of that and as real as it sounded, I stayed in my own world and prayed and begged God to give me this chance. I begged God every day.

I knew what I was asking for sounded like wishful thinking and I looked like a naïve little 19-year-old who was just playing games with the court system. As serious as things were, I had a glimmer of hope. I don't know where that came from. It was the only thing I had to hold on to. I was scared…really scared. But this hope—this feeling that maybe, just maybe, that's not what God had in store for me—is what kept me sane. Some days I even found joy. Some days I had so much hope that nothing anyone said to me could bring me down or make me think that prison was even a possibility.

I had a Bible and I decided it was time to open it. I am going to be very honest about my use of this Bible. There was an index in the back that would point you to scriptures to read when facing certain subjects like worry, death, fear, addiction, depression, happiness, love—anything you could think of. I picked a few scriptures on worry and fear and those are what I read every day. I did not know much of what was in the Bible. My entire life, I knew that there was a God. I knew that He existed. However, I could not tell you one thing about the Bible. I did not read it growing up or in church.

There were three main passages I read everyday: Psalm 23, Psalm 51 and Matthew 6:25-34. I marked these passages because they talk about trusting the Lord, not worrying, asking to be forgiven, having a clean heart, and asking and receiving from Him. This kept my hope alive. I skimmed the Bible for anything that gave me hope. I was a baby at this stuff. Simple verses, like *"Do not worry* and *Whatever you ask in my name you shall receive,"* are the ones I clung to and stood on. I prayed like never before and I fasted every week.

One morning I woke up to the sound of an officer calling names off a list. "Llop! Pack it up!" I heard. *Pack it up? No. No, no, no!* This was not good. When the officers came up to D-block—the women's block—and started calling names, it usually meant you were being sent to another facility. It was an indicator that your court date was not any time soon and you were in for a long stay. My eyes watered as I got my few belongings together. I heard horror stories of people sent to other facilities, only to get lost in the system with their court case never being put on the court's calendar. Sometimes it was a year or more before they returned to Hall County.

I got sent to Union City and stayed there for 3 months. I was brought back to Hall County with the hopes of my court case coming up soon; that didn't happen. When I got back, there was no word from my attorney, no letter, and no visit. That meant I had no set court date.

As I sat in my cell, just a few days after returning from Union City, I heard an officer come to the door of my cell. "Miss Llop?" she said as she opened the door. It was an officer from the Work Release program, Miss Monica. She was a short, skinny little lady with jet-black hair, freckles, and a tiny voice. I stood up. "Yes?" I answered. My eyes lit up and I smiled. "Come with me," she said. I knew the drill. I had watched it happen many times while I was incarcerated. The Work Release program takes place at another lock-up facility. The participants could leave during the day to work a regular job and would return to the facility at night. The officers give you a drug test , and if you passed, they would take you to "work release."

I walked with her down the hall and she asked, "Would you like to be a house lady at work release?" A house lady is one that comes to work release to work inside at the facility— not outside. Those positions are only for women with more serious charges. My charge was considered a serious charge. The "intent to distribute" charge makes me more than just a drug user. It makes me a drug dealer, and that is highly frowned upon in the criminal justice system. Sentences for charges like that are longer and harder.

I smiled with an excited voice said, "Yes!" I was getting out of a 22-hour lock down and going to a facility with much less security and the freedom to walk outside whenever I wanted. I could now walk outside, with barbed wire fencing all around, but at least I could lie in the grass, look at the sky, and breathe fresh air! We slept in dorms, so nobody was locked in tiny rooms. It was glorious compared to the county jail. *Thank you, God. Thank you, God.* All I could think was, *Thank you, God!*

It was much easier to deal with being incarcerated in this place. However, I still cried many days. I worried. I prayed and fasted. I begged God to have mercy on me. I spent so much time thinking about every way I had smacked God right in the face. I was so sorry. He had done good things for me and opened beautiful paths for me whenever I decided to do the right things. God blessed me with a full paid college scholarship to the school of my choice and with all the life-long friends I made at Boys Town. I thought about the dreams I used to have when I was young. I thought about that *still small voice* I heard when I asked Jesus to come into my heart—that still small voice that was so easy to brush off and ignore. I thought about the times I was on the street in dangerous situations and I could have easily died, but God had better plans for me. I thought about every prayer I prayed. God always seemed to answer them. He never let me down or disappointed me. *What is wrong with me?*

I knew God heard me. I never questioned if my prayers were being heard. I only questioned what God had in mind. Did He really think prison was best for me? Were these prayers going to be answered? Or was He really, really angry with me? When I was 12 years old, God showed Himself to me. From that time on, I *knew* there was a God. I had always believed in God as a child, but when God *shows* you He is real, there is no denying it. He is undeniable. I knew God felt every pain in my heart and saw every tear. I wasn't just sad about being incarcerated. I was a sad person inside. I was a drug addict. I came from a broken home. I was abandoned—both physically and emotionally—by both of my parents as a child. I never accepted the help that was offered me for many years.

I am a hardheaded girl, a stiff-necked person. I had a bad habit of making things in my life a lot more difficult than they needed to be. Yet, I held on to those moments that God was real to me in my life. I held on to that glimmer of hope. I had to pray my way through this. I prayed without ceasing and knew that God heard me. It was the only choice I had. Sitting back and accepting that I was going to prison was not a choice for me.

The days being incarcerated were hard. They were long. I would go long periods of time without seeing my attorney. The few times I saw him, I would get excited and think that my court date was around the corner. No such luck. He just came to update me on where the district attorney was in the negotiating process, which was no progress at all. The district attorney wouldn't budge. I would get that news along with the fact that my court date had not been set on the calendar. "I still want to ask the judge for First Offender's Act," I would tell him every time I saw him. "I'm not agreeing to a prison sentence." Mr. Parr would kindly state, "I'm here to ask for whatever you want me to ask for. It is always better to go to court with a plea bargain, but I will do whatever you want me to do." I could read him. He did not want me to go in to the courtroom, leaving that decision up to the judge. Those meetings were always very discouraging, but I didn't stop praying.

Every morning I would go outside with my coffee and pray. I would look up at the sky and my eyes would fill with tears. I would talk to God. I kept my eyes fixed on the sky when I cried to God; not because I think God is some guy in the sky. I did this to help me realize how small I was and there was a much bigger picture. I also did this to help me focus on the fact that whoever made that big sky, made me, too. My faith went to a new level during this time, despite all of the bad news I was getting from the only person that could help me—my attorney. I chose not to focus on what I was seeing and hearing, and only focused on prayer.

Living in an open dorm where there was no privacy, I would go into the bathroom many days that I started feeling hopeless and fearful. I would close the door behind me, fall on my knees, and sob and pray. I would pray with all of my might. This is all I did for nine long months.

One cold Sunday evening in February, an officer came to get me. "Your attorney is here to see you," she said. I knew it was time. It was

Sunday night. Why else would my attorney be here?

"Your court date is tomorrow morning at 9:00 a.m.," he said. As relieved as I was to finally hear those words after nine months, I got very nervous. Tomorrow was going to be the day. Would my prayers be answered? Was I going to go home after all this time? Or was God angry with me? Maybe His plans were not my plans. Maybe He wanted me to see what prison was like so I would never go down the drug path again. My stomach was in knots.

During the months I was incarcerated, I worked on getting every piece of evidence to my attorney that showed I was better than where I was sitting. I made sure he had pictures, proof of my scholarships, awards, certificates, and proof that I was enrolled in the nursing program and plans to commission into the Army as a Second Lieutenant before I fell into a state of drug addiction. The case we were pleading was that I was a smart girl and a good person that fell off track in life and needed help. There wasn't much else to say.

"The DA (district attorney) is going to go in there tomorrow morning and ask the judge to send you to prison. You still want me to ask for First Offender's Act?" he asked. "Yes," I said. He looked at me for a moment and with all sincerity and curiosity he asked, "Why are you so sure the judge might give you First Offender's Act and let you go home?" I smiled and said, "Because I've been praying about it for nine months." The look on his face changed. He seemed to be very surprised by my answer. His face softened and he smiled. "Okay," he said. "See you tomorrow morning."

I woke up the next morning and the first thing on my mind was God. He was either going to show up in that courtroom and send me to prison, or I was going to watch a miracle unfold before my eyes. They only one in this universe that could move on the judge's heart, to not side with the state, was God. I was filled with nerves. My hands shook all morning. I couldn't eat breakfast. I went in to the bathroom one last time to hit my knees and pray.

An officer transported me from the Work Release facility to the court. I sat in the waiting cell to be taken in to the courtroom. I heard the door click and an officer with shackles in her hand stood there. I walked over. She cuffed my hands in front of me. She put shackles on my feet. She opened the door to the courtroom and told me where to go sit. I shuffled across the courtroom and sat down with my attorney.

Judge Girardeu was not the judge residing over my case, which I found a little strange. The judge I was in front of was a retired judge filling in that day. We all stood as he entered the courtroom to take his seat. The district attorney proceeded to the microphone and the court reporter began to type. The proceedings had begun. The district attorney read my name, my charges, and her recommendation for sentencing—8 years with 4 to serve in prison. When it was my attorney's turn, he told the judge a little bit about me before I got arrested in January of 2004. He told the judge where I was enrolled in school, about my scholarships, and a little bit about my achievements in high school (since I was still pretty fresh out of high school). He pointed out that my parents were in the courtroom that day to support me. He did his thing as an attorney and painted a pretty nice picture. The good thing was, it was the truth. He ended with, "We are asking that Miss Llop be sentenced under the First Offender's Act."

After my attorney spoke, the judge looked at me and said, "Miss Llop, would you like to say anything before I make my decision?" I had been mentally preparing for this opportunity. I stepped up the microphone and the speech that flowed from my mouth was something of another power. Still to this day, I cannot remember exactly what I said to that judge. I only remember making it clear that I had plans and a hope for a bright future. I was working hard toward a goal and I let my life spiral out of control with bad decisions. I told him that I had never had so much time alone to sit and think about my life. I went on for quite a while. It was not a short response, by any means. I asked him to please consider giving me one last chance.

In most cases, courtrooms are filled with attorneys, prosecutors, defendants, witnesses, and family members who are all waiting their turn to get in front of the judge. The courtroom I was in was filled with the same. I never witnessed a courtroom as still and as silent as it was in that moment. Everyone had his or her eyes on Mr. Parr and me. The stunned looks on people's faces said, "Wow, are they really trying this?" and "What is going to happen to this girl?"

I finished all I had to say. My Parr and I stood there waiting for the judge to respond. He looked at me for a moment. He didn't say anything for what seemed like an eternity. I was so nervous, I thought I was either going to faint or throw up because God's answer—not the judge's decision—but God's answer was going to be the next thing out of this man's mouth.

"I'm going to have to think about this," he said. "I will reschedule this for 9:00 a.m. Wednesday." Wait. What? This was completely unexpected.

As I was escorted out of the courtroom, Mr. Parr followed. He told me he would see me Wednesday morning and that it was probably a good thing that the judge was taking this to heart, thinking about it for a couple of days. One of my persistent daily prayers was, "God, please soften the heart of the judge deciding my case." I took the next two days to press into God and pray some more. It was all I could do.

When I arrived at the courtroom that Wednesday morning, I saw my parents there again. My case was the first one called that morning. A couple attorneys, that were in the courtroom on Monday, came back just to see the outcome of my case. I stood with Mr. Parr by my side. The district attorney stood on her side and we all waited for the judge's decision. The judge looked up at me and said, "I have thought about this and have made a decision. I am sentencing Miss Llop under the First Offender's Act with 5 years on probation and to be released today with time served. Miss Llop, I don't ever want to see you in this courtroom again." I gasped and let my head fall in front of me. My eyes filled with tears. There it was. There was God's answer. God was so real in that moment that I could have touched Him.

"Thank you, Your Honor," Mr. Parr responded. I looked up and smiled at Mr. Parr with eyes filled with tears. My breathing was as if I had just run a mile. He smiled back and we walked out of the courtroom back to the holding area for inmates. When the door closed behind us, I let my tears fall and cried out of relief. Mr. Parr was just as shocked as I was. He shared in my joy. "Congratulations," he said. "Katherine, I work with the youth group at Gainesville United Methodist Church. Would you be interested in coming and speaking to them next Sunday and sharing your story with them?" I was shocked. This guy wants me to come speak at his church? He was clearly moved by the whole experience with me, knowing that I went in that courtroom on faith... and faith alone. "Yes! Yes, I would love to!" I told him. "Great. Give me a call when you get home and we can talk a little more about it," he said. "Thank you. Thank you so much, Mr. Parr," I said. I turned to follow the officer transporting me back to Work Release, feeling light as a feather.

It happened. God showed up! I got exactly what I prayed for, and the thing about it is that nothing like that had ever happened in the history of the Hall County Court system! Nobody had ever been terminated from Drug Court and given a second chance under First Offender's Act. God proved Himself to me once again. There was no other explanation for the miracle in that courtroom. God truly softened the heart of the judge deciding my case. I got exactly what I asked for. God was undeniable that day and I felt His presence stronger than I ever had. The mercy of God endures forever. He is a merciful, loving, and kind God. This I know. At the same time, He is our Father and He *does* discipline. God was not playing around with me by making me sit in jail for nine months. This life is not a joke and God doesn't want *anyone* to perish. He wants all of us to turn to Him and choose life. He is a good, good Father and every promise in His word is true. This was a major miracle in my life. I will never forget that day or those nine long, hard months.

CHAPTER 13

Mr. Alexander

Upon being released, my mother offered to let me live with her. The first morning I woke up at my mother's house, I sat outside as the sun rose and sipped on a chai tea latte, my favorite at the time. I looked up to the sky the way I did for many months and thanked God. I was happy to be free; but I was happier to know that there really was a God. He heard me and proved Himself to me in a new way. He was so real, so undeniable, and all I wanted to do was please Him.

I called Mr. Parr at his office to check in with him about coming to his church. I asked what exactly he wanted me to share and he said to simply share my story and talk about making choices in life. He gave me the address and told me to come that Sunday night. I grabbed some note cards and began planning my speech.

During that week, I spent some time with a friend of mine. We rode around, went shopping, and went out to eat. He asked me if I would mind riding by an attorney's office in Gainesville because he needed to stop by and talk to him. While I was incarcerated, my friend was a witness to an accident. The attorney handling the victim's case retrieved his information from the 911-phone call he made. I agreed. We showed up at a personal injury firm and I sat down while he discussed a few things with the attorney. The attorney's name was Mark Alexander. As the conversation ended and we walked down the hallway to leave, he asked my friend if he knew anyone that needed a Honda. He was selling the car that got him through law school so he could get a truck. My friend asked him how much he was selling it for and told him he would let him know if he knew of anyone that would be interested.

The Sunday I was to speak at Gainesville First United Methodist was an exciting day for me. I was a little nervous to speak to a group of people, but thought, "It's just a youth group. It's probably not that many people." When I got to the church, I met Mr. Parr out front. He walked me in and took me to an area of the church that was packed—and I mean *packed* with youth, adults and, of course, my parents. It was a much bigger group than I had imagined. I sat near the stage and Mr. Parr got up there with a microphone. He told the audience that he had a special guest there that night to talk about *choices* we make in life. He said nothing about representing me in court. He left all of the details of what I wanted to share up to me.

I took the stage and with my note cards in hand, began to openly share about my life. I talked about my life in high school and all of my achievements. I talked about entering the nursing program at North Georgia and my plans to commission into the Army when I graduated. Then, I told how I tried meth one time and how my life spiraled out of control. I could tell I had everyone's attention. Not one face was looking in another direction and everyone was still and silent.

I continued with explaining the darkness of addiction. I told them that I got arrested and continued to struggle and because of the choices I made, I ended up in jail for nine months. I revealed that Mr. Parr was the attorney that represented me. I talked about my time in prayer for those nine months and how I turned my heart to God. I wanted to make it clear that I was not just sorry that I had gotten caught and was in jail. I was truly sorry for the things I had done, the choices I made, and that I really did not want to live that life. I shared with them the miracle that took place in the courtroom earlier that week and that it was only by the grace of God that I stood before them, urging them to keep God in the center of their lives. It was a story of a girl that messed up, turned to

God, and was given a chance to get it right. I was just trying to pick up all of the pieces and get my life back together. Everything in our lives comes down to the *choices* we make.

As I ended my speech, I thanked Mr. Parr for having me there and I put the microphone down. Everyone stood to their feet and gave me a big round of applause. I saw my father standing all the way in the back, smiling. He clapped and I could see a sense of pride on his face. I smiled and humbly walked off the stage.

When Mr. Parr closed the meeting, everyone arose from his or her seat and stood in line to shake my hand, hug me, and tell me "thank you." After shaking and hugging what seemed like a hundred people or more, I headed for the exit. As I was walking I felt a tap on my shoulder. I turned around and it was Mr. Alexander, the attorney I just met the other day with my friend. "Small world," I thought. "Hello," I said in a shocked tone. "Hi, Katherine. Do you remember meeting me the other day?" he asked. "Yes, I do!" I said. "That was a powerful story you shared tonight. Thank you for coming and sharing that. I also work with the youth group here," he said. "Would you mind coming to my office Monday morning? I'd like to talk to you about something." "Sure, I can do that," I told him, thinking maybe he would elaborate while we were standing there. I waited for him to keep talking. "Okay, great. See you tomorrow. Just give me a call when you are on your way," he said. I had no idea what this was about, but I smiled and told him I would see him tomorrow.

The next morning I had my friend pick me up to give me a ride to Mr. Alexander's office. I walked inside the building and told the lady at the front desk who I was there to see. I waited for a moment and saw Mr. Alexander coming to get me. "Hi, Katherine! Come back to my office, if you don't mind," he said. I followed him in to his office. He closed the door and stood next to his desk. Since he was standing, I stood, too. He began to speak and about three words into his sentence, he began to get choked up. His eyes began to water. He said, "Katherine, when I was standing in the back of that room listening to your story, I felt God so strongly. I felt like God was speaking to me and I'm not even a very spiritual man. (This is not still not the case for Mr. Alexander.) I felt like God was telling me that you really need my car and that I need to give it to you."

As I stood there listening to Mr. Alexander, I could not help but to become emotional myself. What was happening was unbelievable! Mr. Alexander did not know that my stepmother had helped me get enrolled in school again and I did not have a way to get to my classes. Also, one of the things required of me on First Offender's Act probation, was to be employed. I had no way of going out and looking for a job. My eyes filled with tears and I stood there and cried in his office. "What? Are you serious? Oh my…thank you! Thank you so much!" I said through tears. I couldn't believe what was happening. He wiped tears away from his eyes and picked up a pen on his desk. "Okay. Now tell me your full name," he said. On his desk was the title to his car and the keys. He wrote my name on the title, signed it over, and handed me the keys. He walked me down to his car to show it to me. It was a black, two-door Honda Civic with wood grain interior. It was in really good shape. I couldn't stop thanking him while we stood there. I gave him a hug. As he walked away he said, "I'll be checking up on you. Don't let me down!" "I won't! Thank you so much, Mr. Alexander," I said. I got in the car, still in disbelief, and drove away.

The last thing on my mind was obtaining a vehicle when I came home from jail. I expected to bum rides from anyone who would take me where I needed to be. I did not think having a car of my own was something I would have for a while. However, God knew I needed that car. God wasn't going to stop in that courtroom. God will always keep showing up if you make Him the center of your life. He knew I wanted to get my life back and wanted me to have whatever I needed to make that happen.

God didn't give me the car through a family member or a friend. He didn't provide money for me to buy a car on my own. No! God did it His own way, which was different from the way I would have imagined things happening. God provided a car for me. He moved on the heart of a man that did not know me, to *give* me his car. God wanted me to know, without a doubt, that He provided that car. God also wanted to move in Mr. Alexander's life. I strongly believe that God wanted Mr. Alexander to step out in faith and trust that it was God's voice that he heard. I was not the only one blessed that day. I truly believe that by blessing me, Mr. Alexander received a huge blessing as well.

CHAPTER 14

Healing of the Heart

My father reached out to me and told me about a friend of his named Kathy. He told me that she was very in tune with the Spirit and thought she would be a good person for me to talk to. He said that she had spiritually helped him and my stepmother tremendously. I wasn't the kind of person to open up and talk to people (ever). I was hesitant, but agreed to give her a call and give it a shot. After all, I had nothing to lose.

The first time I met with Kathy, she was not what I expected—not religious, but very spiritual. She was tall with long, curly hair and a beautiful smile. Her voice was soothing and I immediately felt comfortable around her. Even though I felt comfortable around her, I really didn't want to go way back in my life and talk about my past. I didn't want to admit to myself that I had problems. I didn't want anyone to think I felt sorry for myself or felt like a victim. For so long, it was easier to just put on a smile, stay busy, and ignore anything going on deep inside myself from my childhood. I didn't want anyone else to think I needed help, so I always put on a façade.

That is how I felt with Kathy, too. I put on a big smile when I talked to her and acted like I was happy. In reality, I was good at being happy on the surface. I was very happy that God worked a miracle in a courtroom for me and then told a man that didn't know me to give me his car. Those were definitely *God moments.* I was in a good place, at least on the surface, and this was how I got through life. I always convinced myself that I was fine.

Kathy said, "So tell me about yourself! I hear you were at North Georgia on some scholarships. Your father was really bragging about you." I thought, "*My* father was bragging…about *me*? That's odd." I never in a million years thought my father was proud of me. I put him through a lot when I was running away from home, getting arrested, shaving my head, and participating in other "interesting" events in my life. Because of how emotionally distant he was, I never thought he would brag about me to someone else.

I told Kathy about North Georgia and how I ended up there. I told her about high school at Boys Town and she stopped me there. "What brought you to Boy Town?" she asked. "Of course…here we go," I thought. I told Kathy that I got sent to Boys Town because I kept running away from home. I ran away from home because I didn't feel loved at home and went looking for it myself. I told her that I didn't feel loved at home because nobody paid attention to me. I told her my mother literally left me when I was seven years old and my father never gave me hugs, never took me to buy clothes, never asked me how my day was, never did homework with me, never spent time with me, or did anything else of that nature. She asked a lot of questions along the way to understand more and get a good sense of *why* I just got released from a nine month stay in jail and completely threw away the ride I had going on at North Georgia. She was trying to understand my self-sabotaging behavior.

As I told Kathy about my life, I did what I always do when I have to get honest. I got nervous. Dishonesty was a defense mechanism of mine for so long. I never laid my life story out for someone the way I did with Kathy. The only thing I could do was wiggle my foot and look around as I talked to her. I was nervous, but I let it all out. I don't know where that level of honesty and bravery came from, making myself so open and vulnerable. I suppose it was just time.

The conversation became focused on my mother. It was clear that

God wanted to address my mother that day. I shared how my mother left when I was seven years old and I relived those moments when I was a little girl. I felt bad for that little girl that didn't understand why her mom didn't want to be with her anymore. I relived my mom giving me the Whitney Houston tape for Christmas with the song, "*I will always love you,*" on it. That was her way of saying goodbye. I remember crying when I felt her cry that morning as she said goodbye. I relived her telling me, with no emotion at all, that she was moving to Florida with her new husband. I relived the first feelings of rage and confusion. *Why are you leaving me? What have I done to make you not love me anymore?*

Then Kathy said, "Ok, it's time. Jesus wants to reveal the truth to you. He is here right now. Do you want Him to heal you? "Um…yes," I said, not knowing what she was talking about. "Jesus?" I thought. I, still at this point, was not 100% clear about the God/Jesus thing. I didn't know why we were involving Jesus in this. I remember as a child, sitting in Catholic church, looking up at the enormous crucifix hanging from the ceiling over the altar and thinking, "Jesus—something about that guy seems right so I won't toss Him out just yet." Even the moment I had at Boys Town with Kerry, my family teacher, when I asked Jesus to come into my heart was a little bit confusing, even though it felt right. I wasn't exactly sure what the difference between God and Jesus was. All I knew was that it felt right. It had always felt that way my entire life. I held on to this belief that there was *something* about this Jesus guy.

"What do you hear Him saying to you?" she asked. "Wait, I am supposed to listen for Jesus to talk to me right now?" I was confused. This was all new to me and I didn't know what I was listening for. I was also filled with so much emotion right then that I couldn't concentrate. I couldn't get past what I was feeling and something was trying to stop me from hearing. It felt like I was sitting in the middle of a battle. It was very strange. I could feel it in the air and it made me mad. I shook my head and rolled my eyes. I was frustrated.

All of a sudden, I heard Kathy start talking but I remember not feeling like it was Kathy talking. From the first word that came out of her mouth I thought, "This sounds…or feels…familiar." She was talking to me in a way that made me feel like she had known me my whole life. This was the first time I ever experienced the Spirit of God speaking to me through someone.

She said, "You're mother has always loved you. The way she handled the divorce was the only way she knew how. She made bad decisions, just like you make bad decisions. She is human, just like you." Those words (which, by the way, were not Kathy's) penetrated so deep in my spirit, that I was caught off guard and didn't know what was happening or how to handle it. I had heard those words before, but this was the first time the words penetrated my spirit, giving me *understanding*. It was an instant download of information. It was a solid "knowing" in my spirit—a divine revelation. It happened in an *instant* and was extremely powerful. When you receive a revelation directly from God, there is no need for explanation. It is a full, instant understanding. Tears rapidly began flooding my face and I cried the most cleansing cry I had ever experienced deep from my spirit. It was uncontrollable. What shocked me the most was realizing I was not crying tears of sadness, at all. It was a cry of relief and joy.

I kept looking at Kathy as I was crying and giving her a look of, "What is this?" and "Do you know what is happening to me right now?" As I was crying, I remember feeling from my chest and stomach area something *literally come out* of me. Something left me. Something physically left my body and I could *literally feel* something *rock solid* come in its place. It was like a heavy brick was placed in my spirit that could not be moved.

Then, it was over. I stopped crying and I had a big smile on my face. It was the strangest thing I had ever experienced. It was also the best thing I had ever experienced. None of what had just happened made sense or seemed believable.

The next moment was just as supernatural as the cleansing cry I had just had. In an instant, my mother was not a selfish, cruel person to me anymore. It was like someone had taken a pair of glasses off that

I had been wearing for a long time. I could see my mother so clearly. I saw a human being that had pain and hurt and made bad decisions—just like me. I saw my mother who held me and hugged me and smiled when she stepped back to look at me after she dressed me and did my hair when I was little. I saw the mother that kissed my face ten times in a row and bit her lip when she hugged me as tight as she could. I saw my mother that would sit and listen to me count to 100 and show her how I learned how to write all of my ABC's. I saw my mother that got joy out of preparing bubble baths for me. I also saw another imperfect human, just like myself.

All of a sudden, I saw my mother in a different light. I saw so clearly how much my mother loved me and how quickly her behavior changed during the divorce. My mother was hurt. She had so much pain and dealt with it in a reckless manner that affected my entire life from that point on. Most of all, however, I felt bad for my mother for the first time in my life. I felt bad that she was so distraught and had such bad coping skills that caused her to abandon her children and emotionally detach from us. It was the only way she knew how to deal with things back then.

I looked at Kathy like, "Who are you and what has just happened, because I need some more of that!" It was a miraculous moment. So many false ways of thinking and lies had been replaced with truth. One by one, the holes in my spirit began to close and I felt a sense of wholeness. I saw the world in a completely different way. My mind had been renewed in an instant and the lenses I saw the world through, came off.

You might think this sounded like a regular counseling session where someone told me some things that should have been obvious. This was not the case. It might sound simple, but I had been told these kinds of things many times. It was much different to experience something being spoken—declared—into the depths of your spirit. What I heard was not heard with my ears. It was heard from the inside with spiritual ears. It was a revelation of truth, directly from this Jesus guy!

When I went home, I felt like I was walking on air. I felt light and free. I had a smile that wouldn't go away. The world literally looked different to me. Many things were so different that day. I looked at my mother and saw a human being that was on her own journey. Love spilled out of me. I wasn't mad at her. Forgiveness happened, yet forgiveness is a small word compared to what really took place between my mother and I. I had worth and value. Nothing could change the truth that invaded my spirit. It was solid as a rock. Lies that had formed holes in my spirit had just been filled with something that felt like spiritual bricks. It was real and it was there to stay.

I met with Kathy quite a few times after this. We talked about my father and the situation was similar. The lie that I believed—that I was a big inconvenience and not worth his time—was replaced with the truth. I began to experience revelations directly from Jesus. The more I did this, the more the holes in my heart healed. I stepped more and more into a state of freedom.

I received the same revelations about my father and truth about him that I received about my mother—he's a sinner, too—just like me. Jesus told me that the things from my childhood that made me feel unworthy of love are why I sabotaged every good thing that came my way. I didn't think I was worthy of anything good in life, especially since I wasn't worthy of being loved by the ones who were supposed to love me the most.

Jesus was ready to tell me the truth about the root of all my issues. I did not believe I was worthy of anything good. I did not believe I was worthy of love. Love is what we were created for. I lived a life subconsciously trying to destroy myself because I believed this lie. In that moment, Jesus spoke to my spirit something that might sound so simple to some, but was so life changing for me. He said, "You are so worthy of love that I died on a cross for you." I took in a deep breath and felt everything inside myself spill out. Tears flowed from me, uncontrollably. Again, I felt something heavy and deep within, literally *leave* me. I cried a happy, cleansing cry, and my spiritual eyes were opened even more.

It was another download of truth into my spirit. A fog was lifted. I saw my life in a way that I had never seen it. I saw myself the way God saw me. I realized who I truly was—HIS KID! The Creator of the universe always loved me. He had been with me, speaking to me, and protecting me for as long as I can remember, in spite of the bad decisions I made. I was created to experience His life in me this way!

The healing of my heart was the most supernatural thing I had ever experienced. It made me a new person. I saw the truth about everything that had ever happened to me. It was liberating. I thought dreaming about future events was supernatural. It was nothing compared to what happened in my heart. It was nothing compared to the miracle of instant healing and supernatural downloads into my spirit. The healings were so complex. They were so *deep*. There was so much to my past and so many issues that needed to be addressed. However, I found out that when God works miracles, they are instantaneous!

I was invited to my father's house for a get-together a few weeks after this amazing healing took place. I hadn't told *anyone* about my conversations with Kathy or what I had experienced with Jesus. I didn't feel like I needed to. I also did not think anyone could understand the depth of what I was telling them even if I tried to explain what had happened. Or would they even believe me? Even now, writing this, I feel like words do no justice to what I experienced. Spiritual matters are hard to put in to words.

While I was at my father's house we went to the basement to get something. As we started toward the stairs, my father stopped me and he said, "Katherine, I want to say something to you. I want to tell you that I am sorry I wasn't there for you when you were little."

I looked at my father and with a big smile I said, "Dad, it's okay. I know you were just doing the only thing you knew how to do. You're a human just like me and we all make mistakes. It's okay. I love you." There were no tears. I did not get sad or upset. I felt pure peace with those memories. That is when you know you have truly been healed—when you no longer feel pain associated with memories. I responded with love. I responded with a heart of forgiveness. It was a beautiful moment. We hugged and he said, "Thank you." I know it was a moment of healing for him, too. This was true freedom. God's timing is always perfect.

I was walking in pure truth and real freedom. I literally felt like spiritual chains that connected me to the idea that getting high would solve my problems, had been broken. I had inner freedom from thoughts of worthlessness and being unlovable. It was absolutely amazing. It was pure joy. The joy had nothing to do with my circumstances or anything going on around me. It came from within. It was perfect shalom—peace and wholeness. It was supernatural. Jesus had swung the prison door wide open for me. All I had to do was walk out.

CHAPTER 15

A Continuing Theme

With the help of my father and stepmother, I enrolled back in school. They paid for all my classes so that I could focus on getting back on my feet. The car that Mr. Alexander gave me enabled me to get to my classes and my job. I did everything that was requested of me by the courts. Life was getting back to the way it should be—healthy and without chaos.

I resided with my mother during this time. It gave me a sense of stability and comfort. Everything was always clean, warm, and cozy. Mom always kept a meticulous, beautiful home. She prepared the most wonderful meals for us to enjoy. We spent time together. The time I spent with my mother was so different from any other time. I was able to be myself and accept every little thing about my mother and who she was. My new heart towards her was nothing short of a miracle. There was no animosity, no tension, and no hard feelings. It was beautiful. God opened my eyes to see that my mom is on a journey, just like me. That's exactly how God wants us to see everyone in our lives.

Many times my mother brought up how she couldn't believe she left my brothers and me when we were little. She apologized over and over again. She assured me that she loved me. She wanted me to know that I was always her little girl and that she worried about me when she was away for so long. The old me would have felt rage. The old me would have cried and told her how hard she made my life. There was no need for any of that. I was able to tell her the same things I told my father—that I forgave her and it was really okay! I told her that I knew she was dealing with everything the only way she knew how. "Mom," I said, "we all make mistakes. I know that you always loved me. It's okay!" She became very upset and cried every time she brought up the past and began apologizing all over again. I wanted her to know that she was forgiven. The apologies went on for years. However, I was at peace when my mother brought these things up. God's timing, again, allowed me to be in a place to assure her that I was not angry with her anymore. It was exactly where God wanted me to be when my parents finally apologized.

One evening, my mother and I got in a terrible fight. She asked me not to have a person over to her home and I did anyway when she was out of town. She lost it on me. I was completely thrown by how she was reacting. I understood her being upset, but she acted like I had burned the house to the ground. I didn't understand how she could be so mean and say the cruel, hurtful things she said to me. I thought we were in a different place in our relationship. I didn't think she was able to hurt me the way she was hurting me in that moment. She got in my face and yelled and told me to leave her house and never come back.

I was in total shock. I didn't know what to do or how to act. I thought that things like this weren't supposed to happen after what I had been through. I thought everything in life was supposed to be easy from here on out. I didn't think words so mean and awful could possibly spill out of her mouth to me. It cut deep into my heart. I was confused. *Why am I feeling this way? Why is this happening? I thought she was sorry.*

I cried and ran upstairs to my room. I grabbed some clothes, got in my car, and left. I drove a few miles down the road and had to pull over in to a church parking lot. *What just happened? How is this happening? Why?* I sat in the parking lot and cried. I had nowhere to go. I had no idea what to do next. A fog came over my mind and all I could think about was how angry I was that my mother, who I had forgiven and loved, had just treated me the way she had. I felt a burning sensation in my chest and anger boiling up inside myself.

I picked up my phone and scrolled to the name "Duff." Duff was someone I used drugs with in the past. Duff was someone I knew sold on the side to support his own habit. His house was always open to users and it was the only place I could think of going to. *Stop, Katherine. What are you thinking? You want to go get high? No, you don't. No, you don't.* I sat there for another minute, stared at his number, and then looked around the empty parking lot. I went into a daze and replayed everything that had just transpired at my mother's house.

I looked back down and slowly brought my finger to my phone to press, "send." Twenty minutes later I arrived at Duff's house. I walked in and I knew every face in there. "Kat! What's up? Where ya' been? Dang, I haven't seen you in a long time! What's been going on?" they all asked. I sat down, got high, and turned my back on everything.

This began the longest stretch of drug use ever in my life. I went deeper into the drug scene than I had ever been, and got in more trouble than I ever had. I completely lost it. I remember time and time again thinking to myself, "I know what I am doing. I know that I will probably end up back in jail. I have turned my back on God. I do not want to do this, but I'm doing it anyway. Screw it." Why? What is going on here? How could I do this after everything I had just been through? There were so many conflicting thoughts and feelings. I did not get high because I needed an escape or to make me feel different on the inside. I was not trying to fill any voids. I didn't have any voids. I chose to go get high simply out of hurt. That had been my response to everything in life for so long. I sat in a parking lot and made a *choice* that night.

I lost everything. I stopped responding and doing what I was supposed to be doing on probation. I didn't report to my probation officer or pay any of my fines. This resulted in a warrant being put out for my arrest. I stole from people and people stole from me. I went on living the life of a drug addict, running the streets. I got so deep into drug use and became so depressed that on my twenty-second birthday, I had

121

nowhere to go and was walking along the side of a road in a town I was unfamiliar with. I thought how nice it would be if a car hit me and took me out of this world. I will never forget having that thought. I had never wished for my life to end; but that day I did. It was the lowest point I had ever been—mentally and spiritually. I did not want to live anymore.

I had gotten myself into so much trouble, and made such a big mess out of my life again, that the only thing I could think of was to run as long as I could. It was all I knew to do.

I put myself in very scary situations again. One evening, I was at a drug dealer's apartment. There were three other people in this apartment. I was sitting in the front room and the others were sitting in the back room. The drug dealer told us that he was going to make a run and would be back in a little while. Minutes after he left, there was a knock on the front door. I walked over to open the door to see who it was. I knew the people that were always in and out of there, so I thought nothing of opening the door to see who was there. Right when I unlocked the door and turned the handle, someone on the other side burst into the apartment. Another man followed him in. They both put their guns up, walked in, and began yelling, "Where the (explicit) is Nate! Where the (explicit) is he!" My heart felt like it was going to jump out of my chest. They began running though the apartment looking for him. I recognized one of them and had seen him at this guy's apartment buying drugs before. Both of these guys were in bad shape. I could tell they were strung out.

As they walked to the back of the apartment, I ran to the front room and closed the door. I tried to lock it as fast as I could. The handle turned from the outside and the guy I recognized came in with a gun and told me to sit down. "I don't think so!" he said. I sat down and looked away from him. I didn't know if they were going to shoot everyone in there and then raid Nate's apartment, or what was going to happen. He closed the door behind him, stood in front of it, and stared at me. I never feared for my life the way I did in that moment.

Minutes later, he walked out of the room and I heard the front door shut. *Is that it? Are they gone?* I walked to the back of the apartment and the people that were back there were lying on the floor. One popped his head up and looked at me. "Are they gone?" he asked. My hands were shaking and I said in a shaky voice, "They're gone." The rest of the people lifted their heads off the ground and stood up. "What was that? Who were they?" they all started asking. I quickly walked to the front room, grabbed my purse, and ran outside to my car. I hopped in the driver's seat and drove away.

Months after this incident, I was at another drug house. I had been going there for a couple months. I mentioned the subject of "drug houses" in earlier chapters, but would like to elaborate on them so you can have a better understanding of what these places are like.

Drug addicts are constantly looking for their next high. It's all they do. Whether they are selling drugs of their own, or just buying and using, they all look for a "safe place" to get high and stay in as long as they need to. Cars come and go all hours of the night. You can leave for a few days and show back up, knowing you are welcome to come in and stay, get high, make a sale, or do whatever it is you need to do. Until the person that owns or rents that place goes to jail, the place gets raided, you go to jail, or get run off, this is a place you will continue to go to— and it will always be full of drug addicts. After a while, that house will usually go under watch by the police.

The house I had been going to was exceptionally packed out one day. People were all over the place—upstairs and downstairs. I had been there for only a few hours when, sitting in a back room, I looked up from the meth I was holding in my hands to see someone standing in the doorway staring at me. My heart dropped when I saw a badge hanging from his neck. He smiled and motioned with his hand for me to get up. "Come on, honey," he said. I knew exactly who he was. Anyone wearing street clothes with a badge around their neck was the drug task force or undercover cop. The house was in the middle of a raid.

I walked out of the room and followed him in to the kitchen. I saw out the front window five or more new cars parked out front. There must have been six agents in that house. I started shaking and all I could think was, "I'm going to jail. This is it. I'm going to jail again."

The agent began asking me questions in the kitchen. He asked me my name, who I knew in the house, and who I dealt with lately (drug related). "We can take you to jail today or you can help us with something," he said. "Ok," I responded. "Like what?" "We can take you to the office and we'll talk more," the agent said. I left and got in a car with three other agents. We were riding down the road and one of them looked at me and in a very surprised way asked, "You do *meth*?" I nodded my head "yes." "Well, you don't look like it. You don't look like the rest of the meth heads that we see," he exclaimed. "No, you don't!" another one chimed in. "Um, thanks," I said.

When we arrived at the office, all I could think was how to get out of there without actually setting someone up. I was *not* going to set someone up. I didn't feel like getting murdered for being a snitch. One asked to see my phone and I handed it to him. He began looking though my phone numbers and messages. "Awesome! You know "so and so"? Oh, we've wanted him for a while. Help us get him and we won't charge you with possession or put you in jail. Can you get in touch with him now?" I was thinking as fast as I could and said, "Well, you know, I'm sure word has already gotten around to half of the people in this town that you guys just raided "Joe's" house. If I call someone asking them for a large amount of meth they will probably know what is going on. It would probably be better to give it a day. You know, so that they don't get wigged out or anything," I told them.

They all looked at me and thought for a moment. "So, you can come back in the morning? Because if you don't, then we're going to put a warrant out for your arrest," one said. "Oh yeah, I'll be back in the morning," I assured him. "Do you need one of us to pick you up? Here, put this number in your phone and just call us if you need a ride," he said.

I got in the car with one of the agents and asked them to drop me off at a nearby drug store. I called a friend to come get me and take me to get my things from "Joe's." The next day, I took off to Virginia. I was scared and didn't know what else to do. I needed to get out of Georgia.

While I was in Virginia, all I could do was sleep and cry. If I wasn't sleeping, I was crying. I was so thirsty and so hungry. My body hadn't had adequate sleep, fluids, or food in a year and a half. I was having withdraws and was very emotional.

I decided to call my mother and ask her for help. She was very happy to hear from me and acted like nothing had happened between us. "Find a bus station and I will buy you a ticket home. Just come home. I will help you," she told me. So, I found a Greyhound bus station and called my mom with the information for a ticket back to Atlanta. I got on the bus and headed home, just in time for Thanksgiving.

When I arrived in Atlanta, I was so happy to see the Atlanta skyline and the familiar streets. My bus pulled into the bus station late that night and when I exited the bus, I saw my mother standing outside waiting for me. We ran to each other and hugged. Oh, how good it felt to hug my mother! When I looked at her I had no feelings of anger from the argument we had. I looked at her with a clear mind and a clear heart. Even though I had responded to the argument we had in the "only way I knew how," it did not mean that the miracle in my heart with Jesus that day was null and void, or that it never really happened. I didn't even have to think, "I forgive my mom." I forgave my mom when I pulled out of her driveway that day. My way of thinking was the problem. My habitual reaction to challenges was the problem. It was all in my *mind*, not my heart. I received a healing of the heart and was in a process of renewing my mind. The problem was that I am a human, and humans make mistakes—big mistakes.

Shortly after arriving back in Atlanta, I *chose* to find drugs again. I was battling addiction. Period. That's all there was to it. Drug addiction was still a real thing in my life because I kept *choosing* to use.

How could someone who had experienced such a miracle with Jesus continue to use drugs? That is a very good question. What does it take to come out of drug addiction? If Jesus healing your heart isn't enough for you to radically change your life, then He must not be who He says He is, and you must not have really experienced what you thought you experienced. Right? Wrong! That is not the case at all.

Just a few short months of being back in Georgia, I was driving down a road with a couple of people in my car. One person had meth in the car. We had all been doing meth. I was behind a very slow moving car and I decided to hop over to the turning lane to pass them. Right when I passed them and got back in the correct lane, I saw flashing lights behind me.

I pulled over and rolled down my window. I had warrants out for my arrest. The person in the back seat had meth on him. It was a bad situation in every way. I began to think of what name I could give him that would show up clear when he ran it and hopefully get a warning for driving without a license. However, I had a feeling that I wasn't going anywhere else that day but to the back of his patrol car.

"Ma'am, do you know why I pulled you over?" This is the famous first line out of a police officer's mouth at a traffic stop. "No," I answered. "You can't pass in a turning lane. I need to see your license." I told the officer that I had left my wallet at a friend's house. I gave him a name and date of birth to run instead. My hands got cold and my stomach turned as he walked back to his patrol car to run the information I gave him. I turned around and looked at the person in the back seat. "That cop better not find any meth in my back seat." I knew that I was going to jail that day and the car was going to be searched. The last thing I needed was another drug charge. The driver of the car will always be held accountable for anything found in it, unless someone else owns up to anything illegal being theirs. I knew that wasn't going to happen.

Sure enough, the officer asked me to step out of the vehicle. He asked me what my real name was and if there was anything illegal in the car. I went to jail that day on the warrants that were out for me and received another drug charge for something that wasn't even mine. The guy in the back seat had taken what he had out of his pocket and stuffed it in between the seats. The officer found it and I was charged with it.

When I was taken to booking at the jail, the reality of everything I was facing hit me. I was in *a lot* of trouble. I had charges in two different counties at this point and had warrants out for me. I was scared. Having multiple pending felony charges was a bad thing. I also, in a very strange way, had a small sliver of peace and knew that everything was going to be okay. Where it came from, I have no earthly idea.

I sat down in the holding cell. The holding cell is where God becomes the forefront of your thoughts again. Some people call this "jailhouse religion"—where people in jail for committing crimes, all of a sudden, love God and pray to Him to help them get out of jail. People make promises to God saying they will change their lives and never do what they did again. They carry their Bibles around and pray like they've never prayed before. I've been there, done that!

This was not jailhouse religion for me. I felt so ashamed—like such a jerk for what I had done and the choices I made after what had been done for me through Jesus—that I just sat on that bench and simply gave God a "stare." It was a spiritual stare. It was the look on someone's face when they are saying, "I'm a jerk. I have no idea why I did that." It was the look of a teenager getting caught doing something wrong and looking into the face of a disappointed parent. I literally could feel the stare back. I could feel God in that moment. I was looking into the face of the Healer of my heart as I shook my head and shrugged my shoulders and said, "I don't know...I don't know." I was sorry. I was sorry *again*. Let me just say here, it is okay to be sorry *again*. God is a God of multiple chances.

I had no words for God at that time. No words were needed. He knew my heart. He knew I felt like a huge jerk. All I could think about were those moments of pure joy for an answered prayer. I thought about the miracle of Mr. Alexander and his obedience to the voice of God by giving me his car, when God told him to. I thought about my cleansing cries when *Truth* came into my heart and put a spiritual cement block where I had holes in my heart for my entire life. It was the heavy, solid, spiritual cement of the *Truth* that cannot be moved. I thought about the moment I literally felt something leave my body during those healing times and was given a new set of eyes to view the world with. I thought about dream after dream I had since I was a little girl. Some were of future events that did nothing but build up my faith in God so I knew He was real. How can someone have these experiences in their life and continue to make terrible choices? This is the continuing theme of this book—bad choices, disobedience, and a loving God. You might have another book sitting in your house with the same theme in it. We will get to that later.

CHAPTER 16

God Stuff

I sat on the cold, hard bench in the cold, hard, cement jail cell. My eyes filled with tears as I closed my eyes. I took in a deep breath and said out loud and with every deep, strong, real intention in my spirit, "Okay…I'm done." When I said those words with all sincerity and with every intention from the deepest part of my being, something happened at that moment. It was like I turned off a path in my head and headed down a new one, all on my own free will. It sounds short and simple, but that was it. I simply made a *choice*. I was done. I had never told myself that I was truly done. I made a *choice* in that very moment that no matter what was ahead of me, I was going to do whatever it took to make my life normal again. I was not ever, ever going to pick up another drug. It was that simple. It was just a *choice*.

Something very powerful happened the moment I made a choice to be done with the drug life. When I announced to myself and to God that *I was done*, something happened. I know, without a shadow of a doubt, that God delivered me from drug addiction. It did not take a long time to overcome. I was delivered in an *instant* and never thought about what it would be like to use another drug again. I never put another drug in my body from that day forward. The thought of it made my stomach turn. I did not experience withdrawals in the days ahead in jail. It was as if when I made that simple (but big) decision, God said, "Good, because

I have work for you to do," and He delivered me. It was nothing short of another miracle— I was delivered from drug addiction in an instant while sitting in a jail cell. New life always begins with a *choice*. I had experienced healing of the heart and the joy of walking in that healing, but this was the first time I began to experience "choosing life."

This is one of the most important parts of the book—the point where I made a decision within that changed my life forever. It was not a big supernatural event with God that changed my life forever. It was a decision that I made from my innermost being and that decision allowed me to walk in a new direction of my life. I took a new path and God was able to do amazing things, starting with deliverance from drug addiction. You might be wondering if it was the decision I made, or an actual deliverance from something. The answer is—both. I made a sincere decision to quit, and what usually followed in the life of a recovering addict, I did not experience. I did not crave drugs, romanticize drug use in my head, or anything else of that nature.

I spent a month in jail. As much trouble as I was in—in two different counties—I had peace the entire time I was in there. I had no idea what the plan was for my life but I knew deep down inside that God was truly in control.

The attorney my mother hired told me that the prosecutor wanted prison time for me; but I already knew that prison was not part of God's plan for me. Instead, I was released to a halfway house on probation, decided by two different judges in two different counties. A halfway house is drug rehabilitation program where you live in a house with other recovering addicts, work, have a curfew, and attend alcoholic or narcotic anonymous meetings, working a 12-step program.

You constantly introduce yourself and identify yourself as a drug addict. Before you speak in meetings, you have to say, "Hi, my name is Katherine and I'm a drug addict." Everyone will then respond, "Hi, Katherine." Well, that wasn't for me. I was not a drug addict anymore. I was *delivered*! I was no longer addicted to anything and it wasn't something I was fighting or dealing with anymore.

I had the chance to pick up a bag of meth off the floor of a bathroom while I was in this halfway house and get high. It was like the ultimate test to see if I had actually been delivered from drug addiction. When I saw the bag of meth lying on the floor (where it came from, I have no idea), it was like seeing a spider on the ground. I stepped back and stared at it. A disgusted feeling came over me. I picked up the tiny bag, opened it up, and poured it into the toilet. I dropped the bag in, once it had been emptied, and flushed the toilet. I immediately washed my hands and though, "Gross…"

So, I am going to tell on myself here. This might even offend some people in the AA/NA community, but this is the truth. I spent my entire time in that halfway house reading the Bible and praying. I did what the halfway house told me to do and I followed all of the rules, but the 12 steps and meetings have absolutely nothing to do with where I am today. I did not attend meetings and identify as a drug addict. I went to meetings because I had to. Please understand that I am not saying that anyone who identifies as a drug addict and goes to AA or NA meetings is weak, wrong, or doesn't know God. I believe I was blessed with deliverance so that I can tell others that there *can be* deliverance and you don't have to fight addiction the rest of your life. Someone I am very close to works the 12 steps and attends meetings regularly. Some people need that network and it works for them and there is nothing wrong with that. I believe God is in those meetings. However, there is nothing God can't deliver you from either.

The decision I made to change my ways did not come with easy times. I will tell you that I had work to do. I came out of a life in a world of drug addicts. I literally had a hard time carrying on conversations with people sometimes. I hadn't had a normal conversation with someone in a very long time. Believe me, conversations between people high on drugs were nothing less than strange. I didn't know what sober people talked about. I had just come out of a very dark, low way of life. I knew my worth in a spiritual sense, and that I was worthy of a good life, but I felt so behind in life that I definitely struggled with confidence. I was

131

a girl that had been in and out of jail and had an addiction to drugs for the past four years. I didn't finish college. I had felonies on my record. I didn't have any friends. All I had was Jesus. And let me tell you, He took me by the hand and walked me through life every day. Sometimes, He had to yank me off the ground by my arm and maybe even drag me through some circumstances when I just couldn't do it by myself; but He did not leave me.

I would have days when I would think, "I'm never going to amount to anything. What kind of job will I have with felonies on my record? Who would want to be friends with someone like me?" These were the days I would be spiritually "lying on the ground," not wanting to move, and Jesus would drag me along through the day. I held on to Him. I knew I was where I was because of Him. I was not sitting in a prison cell because of Him. I had a healed heart because of Him. He swung the spiritual prison door wide open to set me free and I had finally made the decision to walk out. Days were hard for me, but I never let go of Him and He never let go of me.

I had spent years and years of my life putting myself through a real, living hell searching for something. The early days I spent on my new walk with God, like I said, were very hard. There were many times I was faced with things that in the past would have sent me to the drug dealer's house. Those were the times I allowed myself to feel emotions and still *chose* to keep walking because I knew the Healer and Deliverer was right there with me. Those were the times I would cling to Him the hardest. The longer I walked with Him, the easier things got. The more I walked with Him, the more I began to realize that He had always been there, even in my sin. Even in my darkest days, He was there. The tears I cried throughout my life, He counted.

The love that I looked for in others, I found in Jesus. The peace that I sought through a temporary high on drugs, I found permanently in Jesus. The joy I sought and the voids I tried to fill were found in Jesus— the Way, the Truth, and the Life. Everything I was looking for in life, I found in Jesus.

There is no one on this planet that will ever be more constant than Jesus. He is my constant. He will never fail me. He is my rock and my light. He will provide for me. He will pick me up when I fall. He will fill my spirit with life. He will be the one watching as I walk in victory and be the one cheering me on. It is in Him that I am able to walk in victory to this very day.

I am here to tell you today, that I did it. I overcame with the Overcomer. Has my life been perfect since I began my walk with Jesus? No. Having Jesus in your life does not mean that your life is going to be perfect, but it does mean that you know who to walk through this life with. You can trust Him. He has never, ever let me down when I put my trust in Him.

New life has brought many amazing things my way. I have seen things from years ago in my life come full circle. I continue to have those dreams that are so special between God and I that strengthens my relationship with Him. I still experience the power of prayer and fasting. I have received words of prophecy that have come to pass. Life is nothing short of amazing with God.

In 2010, I was given a word from a girl that I never met. I was at a church in Atlanta and a kind, young girl told me that she had a word for me from God. She smiled at me and said, "I see you dancing, and the Lord is very pleased with it." I smiled back at her and was encouraged but didn't understand fully what that was about.

As time went on, I became very interested in a certain kind of dance called Davidic dance. This is a Jewish form of worship dance. I would watch videos on the Internet and teach myself dances in my living room. I have always been very drawn to the Hebrew roots of the faith in Jesus as the Messiah. Part of my spiritual journey has been seeking to follow the way the original church was, with all its Jewish roots and foundations. I found teachings from Messianic rabbis, which really spoke to my spirit more than any other teachings. I developed a love for Israel. I already loved Jewish people because I grew up with Jewish families. Something about my love for Israel and Jewish people was supernatural, though. I wasn't sure where this deep, deep love for Israel and the Jewish people came from, but I knew it was there. The answer for this came later in my journey.

I moved to a new neighborhood and found a church that I made my home church. I trusted the pastor and came to find out, this church was a huge supporter of Israel. I am sitting in a service about two months after I began attending and a dance team came out during worship and ministered with dance. I was amazed! I immediately asked how I could join the dance team. I could feel God smiling at me with joy when I asked about this dance team. He knew the desire of my heart to worship Him with dance and He led me to the only church in that area with a dance team. After being on the team for a year, I was asked if I would become the director of the dance team. In this moment, I remembered the word that young girl had given me a couple years before this. "I see you dancing, and the Lord is very pleased with it." This is God stuff. Here is a great example of walking with the Lord and Him giving you the desires of your heart. Put God first, delight yourself in the Lord, and He will guide your steps and give you the desires of your heart.

Another amazing thing happened when I moved to this area. I was driving down the road and ten minutes into my drive, I saw on the right side of the road a big gate with a menorah on it. I slowed down to read the sign and it read, "Beth Hallel A Messianic Synagogue." You have got to be kidding me, God...a Messianic Synagogue ten minutes down the road from my house? In case you don't know, there are not near as many messianic synagogues as there are churches or regular synagogues. There are only a few in the state of Georgia. Again, I felt the Lord smiling down on me.

I began visiting this synagogue regularly on Shabbat (the Sabbath, Saturday). When I experienced the worship during the services, my soul was touched on a much higher level. When I heard the ancient prayers that Jesus heard himself, I felt the ancient power of these prayers and energy flow through my body. I felt a connection in my spirit that I had never felt before.

The summer of 2016, I visited Israel for the first time. It was during that time that I had been in prayer about moving on to Beth Hallel, becoming a member, and raising my children there. One of the things I did while in Israel was have dinner with Holocaust survivors. At that dinner, the rabbi from Beth Hallel and a large group of youth came in. Here I was, in Israel, with my group and suddenly we found ourselves included with a group from Beth Hallel—the very synagogue that I was considering joining! I felt the entire evening was a confirmation that I should move my membership to Beth Hallel. Coincidence? No, this is God stuff.

By the leading of the Lord, I moved on from the church I was attending. To this day, I attend that synagogue, am a member there, and am one of their Davidic dancers.

In 2012, I was walking my daughter through the halls of her new elementary school. Parents were registering their children for the school year. People were everywhere. As I walked through the hall, a woman with an extremely familiar face caught my attention. I slowed down and stared at her. "How do I know her?" I asked myself. I couldn't take my eyes off her. I wanted to approach her, but decided to keep walking. A few months later, I went to my daughter's school again and I heard from behind me, "Katherine?" I turned around and there was the lady with the familiar face. "Yes?" I replied. I still couldn't figure out how I knew her. "I'm Julie Keeton. I was your sixth grade language arts teacher," She said. Everything made perfect sense now that she had identified herself. "That's how I know her!" She didn't look any different than she had many years ago when I sat in her class. She was Ms. Keeton, the one who I openly wrote to in my journal when I started heading down the wrong path in life. Apparently we had been friends on a social network site for a while and I didn't realize it. "Katherine, I have always prayed for you. You were one of my students that I took a particular interest in and have been praying for you for many years. I'm glad to see you are doing so well. It's good to know God answered my prayers for you." Is this a coincidence? No, this is God stuff.

For many years, I thought about Mr. Alexander (the attorney that gave me his car) and what he did for me. I thought about contacting him but could never bring myself to do it. I wanted to simply to tell him that I was thankful and that I would never forget what he did for me. Every time I thought about it, fear of him being angry with me because of the way my life turned out, stopped me from contacting him. "Don't let me down," was the last thing he said to me.

In 2013, I was spending some time in prayer and fasting. The third day into this fast, I was standing on my back porch and I got a very powerful download in my spirit. It was so loud and clear that I even physically felt an impression in my chest area. "Get in touch with Mr. Alexander. Tell him how you are and thank him for what he did for you in 2005." That was the understanding of the download I got in my spirit. My response was "Oh no! No ya' don't! You don't want me to do that. He is mad at me. I just know it." Then, I heard very clearly, "It will bring him *joy* and it will *bless* him." I stood there refusing to do it in my spirit. I was nervous. The thought of actually contacting him and what his response might be discouraged me. This man *gave* me his car because he wanted to help me and look what I did. My life turned into chaos. Again, very clearly and in a strong sense I heard, "It will bring him *joy* and it will *bless* him." I kept hearing this in my spirit as I stood there. Then, I heard, "Now."

I went inside and opened my computer. I got on the Internet and searched "Alexander attorney Gainesville, Georgia." I couldn't remember his first name. I opened a web site and was hopeful that they would have pictures of the attorneys of this specific law firm that sounded like it might be his. I saw "Mark Alexander." I clicked on that name and up came his picture and a short introduction of him on the web site. "Oh, no...I found him." I thought. I was still nervous but was going to be obedient. I couldn't deny what I heard in my spirit. I got his e-mail address from the website and began writing.

Hi Mr. Alexander,

I am excited that I was able to find your contact information! I hope you are well. I'm sure you remember me - you gave me your Honda back in 2005 after meeting me through Ben Jones (who was a witness to one of your cases) and then coincidentally being at Gainesville First United Methodist when I shared my story with the youth group one night (per the request of Dan Parr, who represented me).

I have thought about getting in touch with you many times over the years to tell you how much I appreciate what you did for me. Really. I will never, ever forget it. It is actually a story I share quite often with people. It was another awesome way that God worked in my life. It was so kind of you to do what you did and I know that you were listening to God's voice in that situation. I remember everything you said in your office that day.

Well, let me give you a quick rundown of my life since then...

As I was trying to adjust to living a normal life again, I became busy with being back in school, working and going to counseling. Unfortunately, I did slip back in to old ways. I surrounded myself with old people that were a part of my past and I struggled with addiction again. (I feel terrible telling you this because I remember one of the last things you said to me was, "Don't let me down.") Fast forward to February 7, 2007 - I decided to change my life and do whatever it took to make it happen. I couldn't believe what I had done to my life again. I got into a 9-month program in Atlanta and I never looked back! I went back to school. I completed the paralegal program at Kennesaw State University and went to work for a defense attorney in Marietta. I have two beautiful daughters, Chelsea and Ava. I am now a stay-at-home mom. I live in Marietta and go to Marietta Church of God. I am on the liturgical dance team at my church and couldn't be happier with my life. We bought a house in a beautiful neighborhood that is FULL of children for our kids to grow up with. It's just perfect!

I attached a picture of me and my family from our Disney World trip this past May. Again, thank you for what you did for me. I will never forget it. Be blessed!

Best to you,

Katherine Robertson

I clicked "send" and off it went. I waited a few days and still got no response. "I knew it!" I thought. "He's mad at me! What a stupid idea! I should have never done that. I'll never hear back from him."

Seven days later I received this:

Katherine,

First let me apologize for taking so long to respond. I just was not sure how to respond or what to say.

I still struggle with how to describe to you what a special gift I received from you last week . . . Wow. When I read your email my guts seized up and my heart was filled with a pure, pure __joy__. I am not sure if I have ever felt that before, or felt it so intensely. I'm guessing it's what God stuff feels like.

I am so proud of you and the path you have traveled. You are special. I will never forget you.

"A picture is worth a thousand words." Give everyone in it a big hug. I have kept the picture as a reminder of how He works.

Thank you for __blessing__ me!

Mark

God said, "It will bring him *joy* and it will *bless* him". This is exactly what walking in a life with God is like—stuff like this. Is any of that a coincidence? No. *This is God stuff!* This is proof of an undeniable God! The exact words I heard in my spirit, I read in his email. Tears rolled down my face and I couldn't talk about it to others without crying. It was overwhelming.

God wasn't done with this, either. A couple of weeks later, I received a phone call from Mr. Alexander. He told me that his church asked him to speak one Sunday about a way faith has played a part in his life and he wanted to share this story. He asked if I would mind him sharing this story, including the e-mail. I told him I didn't mind at all. Then, he asked if I would come to the service and read the e-mail myself. Of course, I agreed to.

It was good to see Mr. Alexander and meet his wife who was also involved in the decision to hand over his car to me. When Mr. Alexander began sharing the story one thing struck me. He told the congregation the story of how we met and how God told him to give me his car during the time I was speaking to the youth group there. He said that it was just *days* before I sent him that e-mail that the church had asked him to speak about how faith has played a part in his life. Until then, he had no idea what he was going to talk about. Just a few days later, he received an e-mail from me. What I never told him was that God told me to send that e-mail on the very day when I was fasting. God even said, "NOW." I had no idea, but this is what God wanted Mr. Alexander to talk about. Eight years later, God used this story of faith and how He works.

The week after reuniting with Mr. Alexander and speaking at his church, I received a thank you card in the mail. It read:

Katherine,

Thank you again for your participation in our recent church service. Your presence brought power and meaning to the message. You made that service so special in more ways than one. I hope to have the opportunity to share this

amazing story again sometime.
Take Care,
Mark

And share this story again is what we will do. I have a feeling the final plan for that story is in this book to build up God's people. This is God stuff, for sure.

Daughters of Zion Dance Team.

Delivered! New life in Yeshua!"

CHAPTER 17

Dreams and the Voice of God

As you've read in my earlier chapters, God has shown Himself in some powerful ways in my life. To this day, the most powerful way I still experience God is in dreams. I shared with you the first dream I had when I was 12-years-old at my grandmother's house. My faith in God was solidified that night. God was the only explanation for me having knowledge of things to come. In our humanity, we do not have the ability to know the outcome of future events unless God, Himself, reveals it to us. It is His gift—a word of knowledge.

I know there are psychics and crystal balls out there. People have reported going to psychics and being told things that nobody else knew about. The viewpoints of that psychic can seem real; but where the information comes from is not from God. In Leviticus 19:31, God warns us not to have anything to do with them! *Give no regard to mediums and familiar spirits; do not seek after them, to be defiled by them: I am the LORD your God.* God supplied many spiritual guidelines to protect us, and for good reason. There are many things you can do to open yourself up to darkness. God gave His instructions and guidelines to protect us from such things. God's enemy is a mocker. The enemy can imitate, but he is not the real deal. He is the author of everything that is false and twisted.

I had the *opportunity* to experience false joy, false hope, false peace, false love, imitations, lies, and more lies that were straight from the enemy all through my life. I can now identify many things in my life that are straight from him—attacks that are so obvious. I have also learned to identify fear, like never before. It is a miracle of God's love and mercy that brought me through such dark times in my life, to the new life that I experience with Him. I can honestly say I wouldn't take back any of it since it's led me to where I am today!

God still speaks, in my new life, in the same way He spoke to me in my first dream.

I have all kinds of dreams—warning dreams, dreams that direct me to pray for other people, and some dreams that seem insignificant. However, all of the insights have come to pass.

To give an example of a *warning* dream, I will share with you one that I had in 2012. This dream was about someone I knew that was also a recovering addict. He had run-ins with the law, as I had, and was fresh out of prison for distributing drugs. In the dream, I was looking at him and had an overwhelming sense that he was in a lot of trouble and was going back to jail for a long time. There were no words. It was just an understanding that I suddenly had in my spirit. Then in the dream, my acquaintance said, "They told on me."

The next day, I was standing on my back porch—where I seem to hear from God quite a bit—and I felt an impression in my spirit to pick up the phone and call this person to check on him and give him this warning. I knew the dream I had the night before was that *kind* of dream. In a warning dream, I always feel a specific way, which continues after I wake up. That's when my spirit confirms it is a dream from God.

The next morning I called my friend, but there was no answer. So, I sent a long text message:

> *John, I don't know what is going on with you or what you are up to, but I had a dream last night that someone told on*

you about something you are doing and it sent you back to jail for a long time. I don't know what you have going on but you need to be really careful and stop whatever it is that you are doing. If you are up to no good, you are about to get in a lot of trouble.

Exactly one month later, this person got set up for selling drugs and was arrested again. He went to prison for three years, more time than he had ever done. This was a warning dream, because God wanted him to be warned...because He loves him...even in his sin and wants him to return to Him. Don't ever think God doesn't love a drug dealer, a pimp, or a prostitute. God wants everyone to come to a saving knowledge through Jesus because "we all have fallen short of the glory of God" (Romans 3:23).

I have also had dreams that impress me to pray for people or to reach out to them. Usually, these dreams do not involve words or conversations. These types of dreams are downloads from God to my spirit. I receive an instant *understanding*—a word of knowledge—about the situation.

I had a dream about a family member that I love very much yet only see at holidays and other special events. I had not seen or spoken to this family member in a long time. However, one night I had a dream that I was looking at her and she looked down and depressed. When I awoke, my first thought was to begin praying for her. About a week later, I found out she had just started taking anti-depressants. God wanted me to lift her up to Him in prayer...because He loves her...and wants her to be happy, finding joy and purpose in Him. He wants the same for all of us.

God gave me another dream that directed me to pray for a co-worker. In the dream, a woman I work with said to me, "I have a problem with manifestations." She fell on the floor and lay there for a while. When she stood up and looked at me, I knew I wasn't looking at her. Something else had come up inside her. Her eyes became darkened

143

and I immediately yelled, "Come out of her in the name of Jesus!" Right then, her mouth opened, and she projectile vomited on me. I could feel some of it near my lip. I wiped it away and continued to tell "it" to come out of her. Then I woke up.

The next morning at work, she was not there. When she returned the following day I asked her, "Were you not feeling well yesterday?" and her response was, "Ugh! The devil was in my stomach yesterday." As you can imagine, I was a little shocked by her response because of the dream I had. Then she proceeded to tell me, "It's something I struggle with all the time. I was curled up on the floor, throwing up. I have several health issues." Well, that was a big, loud and clear, "PRAY FOR HER" from God. Everything in my dream lined up with what she told me. I continue to pray for her…because God loves her and wants her well. God gave us a powerful tool called prayer that can work miracles.

The next kind of dream is the most common dream I have from God, and these are the dreams of future events. I have had so many of these dreams, most of which I did not quite understand to be spiritual or have any *Kingdom connection*. For a long time I struggled with why God showed me things that would come to pass even when many of them didn't seem significant. I'm always encouraged and feel connected when I watch the dreams come to pass, because I know that God was communicating with me. The childlike faith in me thinks, "Dad, thank You! Thank You for talking to me! Thank You that You took time to continuously make Yourself undeniable to me because I *know* You are the one revealing these things!" How else could I see things before they happened?

Here are some examples of other dreams that I've had:

I had a dream that I was watching my cousin smile and looking at a ring on her finger. I could feel her joy in this dream. The next month she was engaged.

I had a dream that I was at a restaurant with someone and looked at a plate of food she was eating. The next day, without any plans, I ended up at this restaurant and looked on the table to find her eating the exact plate of food that I saw in my dream.

I have had dreams about seeing someone that I hadn't seen in a long time, and I would run in to that person the next day.

I had a dream that a paycheck did not go into my bank account the day it was supposed to and it was going to be a week late. The next day, the paycheck I was expecting to see deposited, was not there. It was coming a week later.

These are all just a few examples of having dreams about something that would come to pass with no real significance or spiritual message, nor were they *Kingdom building*. *Kingdom building* is a term used when people refer to doing something, or using a spiritual gift, to advance the kingdom of God on Earth. I spent many years confused and wondering, "Why am I not having more important dreams about future events? Why am I just seeing small things happen?"

One of the dreams I love to tell people about may be hard to believe. But it happened. To begin with, I want to go ahead and tell you that I know nothing about the National Football League (NFL). I do not watch football. I do not care about football, and I never know who is going to the Super Bowl until the day of, or a few days prior, to the Super Bowl...until Super Bowl of 2013.

Exactly one week before the Super Bowl, I had a dream that I was standing on a football field and was watching football players with dark purple and blue jerseys running off the field. All were running towards me, jumping and shouting for joy. Some were putting their fists in the air as they jumped and I could literally feel their joy in this dream. It was fun to watch this! I *understood* this team had just won the Super Bowl. The next thing I knew, my attention was directed to the other side of the football field. There I saw a team with red jerseys walking slowly off the field with their heads down, obviously very sad.

The next morning, I didn't even get out of bed, but immediately reached for my phone and called a friend. When he answered I asked, "Who is going to the Super Bowl this year? The Patriots?" He said, "No, the Ravens and the 49ers." I thought the 49ers wore red so I told him,

"I just had a dream that the Ravens won the Super Bowl!" I held on to this and told only close family members. I thought other people would think I was crazy, especially coming from a girl that knew nothing about the NFL.

The night before the Super Bowl, I had another dream that I was standing on a football field again, and watched a player with a dark purple jersey kick a field goal. I *understood* they just made the first touchdown of the game.

For the first time in my life, I had my own mini-super bowl party in my living room. I made dips and other Super Bowl snacks and I sat down to watch the entire game. I *knew* who would win the Super Bowl. The Ravens scored the first touchdown in the first quarter. At that moment, my dream was confirmed. It seemed strange that God would show me something about a silly football game, but I knew it was "that kind" of dream.

I don't know if anyone reading this remembers that game, but in the fourth quarter, it did not look like the Ravens were going to win. I was glued to the screen. I sat there thinking, "God doesn't lie and I know that dream was from Him." Sure enough, the Ravens ended up scoring again, winning the Super Bowl. I could not believe what was happening as I watched the team jump and shout for joy. I shouted for joy in my living room and was amazed that God showed me who would win the Super Bowl that year. I will never forget that game.

Months later, I understood why God gave me that dream. In the spring, I was invited to my neighbor's Bat Mitzvah. I sat at a table with a very outgoing guy that had *lots* of things to talk about, an opinion about everything, and a great sense of humor. He was a friend of the family and I talked with him most of the night. I saw him at the service that morning with a kippa (yarmulke) on. It was clear he was Jewish. During the conversation I asked him, "So, do you go to Temple Kohl Emeth, regularly?" He responded, "Oh no, I'm an atheist!" He was raised Jewish, but was an atheist. The next thing out of his mouth was, "I mean, do you really think God cares who wins the Super Bowl?" What?

Why would he ask such a question? We were not talking about football, or the Super Bowl, or God. I just asked if he went to a particular temple.

My stomach froze, my heart froze, and my brain froze. I knew exactly how God wanted me to respond. I held back. I was nervous and a little intimidated by his strong personality. I didn't want to get into a debate or say, "Funny you say that!" and go into my dream, only for him to not believe me. I thought about it and told myself no. I wasn't going to do it. I didn't know him very well and didn't want to offend him or have him offend me. Even though my Super Bowl dream story is fun and exciting to tell, I couldn't do it. I regretted it every day after that. I missed an opportunity that God gave me to tell someone about Him and I failed.

As I read the Bible, it was comforting to read that God gave many people opportunities and jobs to do, and many times they missed it. However, God stayed with them and still loved them.

During the writing of this book, God spoke to me about that. He told me that this book would fall into every single person's hands that he wants it to. If God wants it to fall into my friend's hands, it will. God has never stopped giving me second chances at anything in life and I am so grateful. Even if I missed an opportunity to talk to my friend about the Super Bowl dream and God, there is still hope that he will hear the Gospel message one day.

You may be thinking, "What is the point of these dreams?" Great question! I struggled with this for years and finally found answers when I opened the Bible. Apparently, God has been speaking to people in dreams for thousands of years so this wasn't something new or unique to me.

Not only does God speak through dreams in the Bible, but He also speaks through people, and speaks directly to us by an inner voice or an impression—even an audible voice or vision—in our waking hours.

God speaks to me in my waking hours, as well. One morning, I was driving down the road on my way to run some errands. I turned off the road my house was on and immediately had a strong impression in my mind. I envisioned two young men, Mormon missionary men, standing at my front door. I saw both of them in their black pants, white short sleeve shirts with name tags, and holding the Book of Mormon in their hands. I had no idea where this thought came from, but thought to myself, "I wonder if Mormons will ever come to my house?"

That same day around 3:30 p.m., I heard a knock on my door. I was cleaning upstairs and my oldest daughter had just gotten home from school. I ran downstairs, expecting to find a neighborhood child asking for my daughter to come out to play.

I opened the front door and to my surprise, there were two, clean-cut, young men in black pants, white shirts, ties, and big smiles on their faces.

"Hi, I'm Elder Anderson and this is Elder Asay and we're with the Church of Jesus Christ of Latter Day Saints."

Before I answered, I had to let my goosebumps settle down. I immediately responded with a big smile, "Whoa! This is crazy that you guys are standing here right now. I was just thinking about Mormon missionaries this morning, and here you guys are, standing at my front door!"

"Oh, really?" Elder Anderson asked with a grin. "What made you think of Mormon missionaries?"

I smiled and replied, "I have no idea." I remember feeling an immediate, strong sense of love toward these boys. Then, I heard in my spirit the word *assignment*, and that was it. I didn't hear any clear instructions. I just knew that God had sent them to my front door and it was my job to talk to them, befriend them, and invite them back. So I did.

I had these two young men, and other young missionaries, come to my house for a month for Bible studies. I grew very fond of these guys. We talked about God, Jesus, and the Book of Mormon. I know their intentions were to get me to the Mormon Church down the road, and to get me baptized in their church. I knew that all along. Each time we met I didn't really know exactly what God wanted me to do. I just knew He wanted me to invite them in and love them. I never planned anything ahead of time. I just followed the leading of the Holy Spirit and welcomed them in my home every week with muffins, cookies, and plenty of decaf drink options.

I read the Book of Mormon, listened to their *teachings*, and asked them questions that they had never considered before. I watched wheels turn in their heads and even offended Elder Asay a time or two. At the last meeting we had, I decided it was time to let them know that their measure of truth was not my measure of truth. Their measure of truth was the Book of Mormon and mine was the Holy Bible. We left each other with prayer and love for one another. It was an amazing month with them.

I have no clear understanding as to the point of those meetings, but I do know some seeds were planted. Elder Anderson had his last meeting of his mission work in my home before he left to go back to Utah. I made sure I sent him with a gift—a t-shirt with a man blowing a shofar and the Aaronic blessing printed on it. I hope he wears it, or at least looks at it, and remembers the questions I asked him. God *showed* me Mormons standing on my front door step hours before they got there. I know the month of "Bible study" with them was from God. I don't know what kinds of seeds were planted, or what will ever come of that. All I know is that God planned all of it.

God has also revealed to me things about people that I could not have possibly known. For example, one evening in church, I was shown a girl abandoned by her father who was addicted to crack cocaine and living on the streets in Atlanta. God showed me He would heal her of that area in her life. Two years later, I heard this young lady gave her testimony at a women's retreat. She talked about her father, a crack addict living on the streets of Atlanta, who she had never known. She is very close to a pastor that picks up people from Atlanta and brings them to church on Sundays, and she calls him "dad." Coincidence? I think not.

One Saturday at a Shabbat service, I sat down in a pew that was directly behind two young boys who were probably about 16 years old.

One boy wore a white kippa (yarmulke) and the other one wore a green kippa, however, my attention was drawn to one in particular. He was tall, thin, and had a full head of brown, wavy hair. When I looked at him I knew instantly that he was going to ask Jesus (or Yeshua—His Hebrew name and what we refer to Him as) to come into his heart at the end of the service. When that time came, Rabbi Kevin (the rabbi of the congregation) told everyone to bow their heads and close their eyes. "If there is anyone here today that has never asked Yeshua to come into your heart and be the Lord of your life and you want to do that today, just raise your hand." I opened my eyes, looked up, and saw that young man raise his hand. You can't make this stuff up.

For many months, God put the urge to write on my heart. I had been reflecting for months on the things God had done in my life. The *impossible* answered prayers, the dreams, the visions, and the impressions in my heart, all came to mind. The undeniable ways God had shown himself to me had been flooding my thinking. My life has been full of God speaking to me and then proving Himself.

God gave me a natural gift of writing. It was the area I excelled the most in while in school. I was the editor of the school newspaper in high school, won awards for my writing, and could write papers in one sitting. I have always loved to write. When the urge to begin writing about the things God had done in my life erupted, I wasn't exactly sure where to go with it.

Without asking God or praying about it, I began moving on my own strength, trying to figure out what to do with my urge to write. So, I started a blog. It was like showering with my socks on. Nothing was flowing out right. I had no idea about successful blogging. I wrote a few blogs, but it just didn't seem right. It was frustrating, to say the least. I knew I needed to get these things off my chest. I knew there was something about the timing of all of this too. I was at a point where my life was so filled with God moving, that I knew it was time to share what God had done.

Finally, I got smart and prayed about it. Genius! I asked God what

He wanted me to do. Suddenly, I began hearing from people that knew me well, "You should write a book." Another person told me, "One day I would love to hear your entire story of how you came to your undeniable faith in God." When I heard a few people say this on separate occasions, I asked God, "Is that what you are telling me to do? Write a book? Ha!" I kind of laughed at the idea. Then God started waking me up at odd hours of the night. My mind would be flooded with all of the stories that are in this book. I *wrote* the book in my head as I lay there in bed, smiling and staring at the ceiling. My heart would be filled with waves of joy.

This went on for a couple of months. I felt like God had shown me exactly what He wanted me to do. If I did nothing else in this life, God wanted me to get my testimony out there. He didn't bring me through so much for me to keep it all to myself. But, write a book? Okay, so it doesn't sound like a challenge since I enjoy writing, but it was a little bit of a surprise. I didn't want to get ahead of myself and jump into this before I knew for a fact that God was telling me to do so. I asked for a very specific confirmation.

I only told one, and only one person, that I thought God *may* be telling me to write a book, but I wasn't totally sure. I didn't speak long about it, and left it at that.

Christmas was just a couple of weeks away and I began praying, asking God to tell me if He was really asking me to write a book. I told God if He was asking me to write a book, then show me with one of my Christmas gifts being something that would help me start writing. I did not have a laptop—or anything else—that I could use when I felt the motivation or urge to write.

On Christmas morning, I received a gift with a note that read, "Maybe this will help you start writing your book." I opened the box to find a tablet with a bluetooth keyboard. I immediately started crying and said, "Hold on. I'm sorry. I'm having a God moment." I could feel His presence in that moment. There it was. Should I have even been surprised? No, but God has a way of never ceasing to amaze me. I received the exact confirmation that I asked God to give me. There was no denying that God had answered me and confirmed He wanted me to write this book. I could not get over the sense of honor I felt that God wanted me to print my testimony for others to read.

Later that afternoon, my good friends from Boston, Tricia and Nick, came over for food and gifts. Nick walked in the living room and as I stood up to greet them, he handed me a big heavy box. I looked at him confused and wondering what in the world was in this box. I sat down unable to smile or show any other emotion because I was just confused at this point. What is this? I opened the box and there was a laptop computer. I looked up at him and he said, "I heard you were going to write a book." Shocked, I sat there and looked down at the laptop and back at him several times. Finally, I got myself together (again), stood up, and hugged him and Tricia, thanking them for the wonderful gift... another God moment, indeed!

God knows I have a problem with questioning His voice and often ask, "was that really You?" So, He knew double the confirmation that day was necessary. There was nothing else I could do at that point but know for a fact—and in an undeniable way—that God told me on December 25, 2014, He wanted me to write a book about what He had done in my life, and how I came to an undeniable faith in Him. So, in January of 2015, I began to write. This entire book was written on the laptop my good friends from Boston gave me.

CHAPTER 18

The Living Word

I am in awe of how far removed I am from the old life I had. Today, I am a new creature. I am a mother of two beautiful little girls. I am a worshipper. Like King David, I dance for the Lord and for all of the wonderful things He has done. I cannot keep silent. When I read in 1 Chronicles 16:8, "Oh, give thank to the Lord! Call upon His name; make known His deeds among the peoples," it pulls at my spirit. This undeniable God has been so good to me; I cannot keep to myself what He has done for me. I know He is real.

I have restored relationships with my family, and have never been closer to my mother and father. It is amazing what God has done in all of our lives. I am glad that God gave me the parents He gave me; I don't know where I would be without them. They are some of my best friends and biggest supporters. Forgiveness, as Jesus taught, is life changing.

Since February 7, 2007, the day I *chose* life, I still had lots of questions about my experiences that I've tried to figure out on my own.

Luckily, due to the fact that the best-selling book in the history of the planet is the *Holy Bible*, it is easy to come by one.. Once I started reading, I was shocked to find so many answers. I would read a passage and think, "Hey, I have experienced this!" or "How did I know that?" or "*THAT* is in the Bible?"

In Chapter 4, I talked about the beginning of my dreams from

God. Apparently, this has been going on for thousands of years and God has been speaking to humans this way for quite some time. In Genesis 37, God spoke to Joseph in dreams. Genesis 37:5-11 reads:

> Now Joseph had a dream, and he told it to his brothers; and they hated him even more. So he said to them, "Please hear this dream which I have dreamed: There we were, binding sheaves in the field. Then behold, my sheaf arose and also stood upright; and indeed your sheaves stood all around and bowed down to my sheaf." And his brothers said to him, "Shall you indeed reign over us? Or shall you indeed have dominion over us?" So they hated him even more for his dreams and for his words. Then he dreamed still another dream and told it to his brothers, and said, "Look, I have dreamed another dream. And this time, the sun, the moon, and the eleven stars bowed down to me." So he told it to his father and his brothers; and his father rebuked him and said to him, "What is this dream that you have dreamed? Shall your mother and I and your brothers indeed come to bow down to the earth before you?" And his brothers envied him, but his father kept the matter in mind.

The story goes on to say that his brothers sold him to some Midianites that took him to Egypt. Joseph experienced hard times, was thrown in jail, and yet eventually was promoted in Egypt over Pharaoh's house and ruled all of Egypt. This promotion came out of his ability to interpret Pharaoh's dreams. God gave Pharoah dreams that Joseph interpreted for him about a famine that would come on the land for seven years. When the famine finally came, Pharaoh knew that God was with Joseph.

There are two things I took away from this story that helped me to understand a couple of things about my own dreams. Even though I was young and didn't fully understand or know all about God, He still gave me supernatural dreams of future events. Even though Pharoah did not believe in the God that Joseph believed in, God still spoke to him through dreams. That cleared up one question in my head—"Would God speak to someone in a dream that isn't *super-spiritual*?" The answer is absolutely, yes! God can speak to anyone about anything, anytime!

The second question that this story answered was, "Why would God give so many dreams about future events that don't seem very spiritually deep, nor do they appear to serve any specific purpose? They seemed to be "nods" from God—as I like to call them—and reassurances that God is with me and is talking to me. Joseph had dreams like this. He dreamed that he would rise up as a ruler and that others, including his brothers, would one day bow to him, which they did. These dreams were strictly for Joseph, and no one else. God used those dreams to build a deeper relationship with Joseph. That is exactly what God has been doing with me since I was 12 years old. He knew what was in my future and the challenges I would face, so knowing Him was something I desperately needed.

We see in Genesis, another way that God spoke through dreams in the life of Jacob. Genesis 28:13-14 says,

> And behold, the LORD stood above it and said: "I am the LORD God of Abraham your father and the God of Isaac; the land on which you lie I will give to you and your descendants. Also your descendants shall be as the dust of the earth; you shall spread abroad to the west and the east, to the north and the south; and in you and in your seed all the families of the earth shall be blessed.

Again, we see God building a deeper relationship with Jacob through a dream that showed him a future event. That dream was concerning the Jewish people, through whom the Savior of the world came. And through this same Jewish nation, and the Messiah who came from it, all the nations who honor Israel have indeed been blessed!

155

When Joseph found out that Mary, the mother of Jesus, was pregnant, he was planning on dismissing her quietly and ending their engagement. In Matthew 1:20-21 we read,

> But while he thought about these things, behold, an angel of the Lord appeared to him in a dream, saying, "Joseph, son of David, do not be afraid to take to you Mary your wife, for that which is conceived in her is of the Holy Spirit. And she will bring forth a Son, and you shall call His name Jesus, for He will save His people from their sins.

Here, God gave a dream with instruction and prophecy in it. God uses dreams for all kinds of purposes, whether they are for instruction, to lead a person to pray for someone else, to warn someone, or a warning for the person praying themselves. I have experienced all of the above types of dreams from God.

I shared with you about the night I asked Jesus to come into my heart after a conversation I had with Kerry, my family teacher at Boys Town. I told you that what I noticed the most about that experience was a very small, soft voice from within that I began hearing. The voice was so soft and gentle, that it was easy to dismiss if I didn't pay attention. In 1 Kings 19, the prophet Elijah had a meeting with God at Horeb. Verses 11-13 say,

> Then He said, "Go out, and stand on the mountain before the Lord." And behold, the Lord passed by, and a great and strong wind tore into the mountains and broke the rocks in pieces before the Lord, but the Lord was not in the wind; and after the wind an earthquake, but the Lord was not in the earthquake; and after the earthquake a fire, but the Lord was not in the fire; and after the fire a still small voice. So it was, when Elijah heard it, that he wrapped his face in his mantle and went out and stood in the entrance of the cave. Suddenly

a voice came to him, and said, "What are you doing here, Elijah?

Elijah heard God as a still small voice. This is exactly how I described and remembered hearing the voice of God the first time. The confirmation in God's Word just keeps coming—more confirmation of the one, true God.

In John 16:5-11 it says,

But now I go away to Him who sent Me, and none of you asks Me, 'Where are You going?' But because I have said these things to you, sorrow has filled your heart. Nevertheless I tell you the truth. It is to your advantage that I go away; for if I do not go away, the Helper will not come to you; but if I depart, I will send Him to you. And when He has come, He will convict the world of sin, and of righteousness, and of judgment: of sin, because they do not believe in Me; of righteousness, because I go to My Father and you see Me no more; of judgment, because the ruler of this world is judged.

When you feel that gentle prompting from within, listen to it. Obey it. That is the work of the Holy Spirit. God's voice is so gentle, it can be easy to ignore. The more you dismiss God and ignore His voice, the fainter it will become.

It is easy to see throughout my story that the enemy kept coming for me. It's a recurring theme. It started in my childhood and continued into college and into my 20s. Right when I got comfortable with life, the enemy knew exactly how to poke at my wounds and stir up false beliefs about myself. He knew where my pain buttons were and how to take me down. I had wounds that the enemy knew were easy targets.

One incident with my mother sent me into a downward spiral and eventually into a deep, dark drug addiction. The wounds from past events that involved my mother brewed some of the biggest lies I believed about myself. Even after the healing miracles I experienced in my heart, the enemy still kept attacking me. You can experience God, experience a miracle, and still choose to turn away from God. The enemy knows that.

In 1 Peter 5:8 the Bible says, "Be sober, be vigilant; because your adversary the devil walks about like a roaring lion, seeking whom he may devour." This scripture could not be truer. I believe that the enemy kept coming for me because he knew I was going to end up doing just this—writing a book about an undeniable God and how many can know Him! He knew I would come out of my challenges with God by my side and I would share with the world all the good things God has done for me. He is the answer to everything in my life. The enemy wanted to stop me from telling this truth.

Earlier, I described a major miracle that happened in a courtroom. I prayed for something that nobody thought could happen. I prayed and fasted for nine months for God to deliver me from a prison sentence that was looming over my head. Everyone thought I was crazy. Yet all over the Bible you will find verses about turning to God in times of trouble. In John 14:13, Jesus told His disciples, And whatever you ask in My name, that I will do, that the Father may be glorified in the Son. He repeats this promise multiple times (in different ways) in the Gospels, urging people not to worry, to pray about everything, trust Him, and believe. I did that for nine months and saw the fruit of that persistent prayer!

I continue to have this kind of connection with God and prayer life. When I pray, I pray without ceasing, no matter how the outward circumstances appear. I believe and I trust. I go to the Father through His Son, His living Word, Jesus, and I never give up. To this day, and without one disappointment, God has continued to be faithful and answer me. I can honestly say from the depths of my heart that God has never ever let me down…not once.

What I described in chapter 14 was a pivotal moment in my life. It is the core of my testimony. When I met Jesus, the Healer, before I even understood what His role and purpose was as the Messiah, my life was forever changed. As I was reading the Bible, I came to a passage in the book of Psalms. I greatly enjoy the book of Psalms because I identify with so much of how King David felt when he poured out his heart to God in prayer, repentance, and praise. Psalm 147:3 says, *"He heals the brokenhearted, and binds up their wounds."* This caught my attention because it is something I experienced firsthand before I knew about this Old Covenant verse.

When I was praying for help with my friend Kathy, she invited Jesus to be a part of my healing, and told me that He was there to answer my prayer. I remember wondering why we were involving Him, but I went with it. You see, because Jesus is exactly who He says He is, He is in the Father and the Father is in Him. In John 10:30 Jesus said, *"I and my Father are one."* He is the living Word of God that took on flesh and came into this world as the Messiah. He healed people. He cast demons out of people. He walked on water and fed 5,000 people with five loaves of bread and two fish. He raised someone from the dead and even told people what they were thinking! "This guy was out of control," I thought! He was not just some false messiah. He was not a liar or crazy. He was exactly who He said He was! He was the Word of God in the flesh, one with the Father, the Messiah!

I could not deny this God that worked miracles for me. I cannot deny what happened to me the first day I experienced the healing of my broken heart and the binding up of spiritual wounds. I had physical reactions to what was going on, and felt *something* leave me (on more than one occasion). I gained a completely different view of the world in an *instant*. I experienced Jesus and His miracles before I ever read about His miracles!

As I continued to read the Bible, I came to the story where Jesus was at the synagogue in Nazareth. He stood up, unrolled the scroll of the prophet Isaiah, and read,

> The Spirit of the LORD is upon me, because He has anointed
> me to preach the gospel to the poor; He has sent me to heal
> the brokenhearted, to proclaim liberty to the captives and

159

recovery of sight to the blind, to set at liberty those who are oppressed; to proclaim the acceptable year of the LORD. Then He closed the book, and gave it back to the attendant and sat down. And the eyes of all who were in the synagogue were fixed on Him. And He began to say to them, Today this Scripture is fulfilled in your hearing. (Luke 4:18-21)

My eyes widened when I read this. I knew and understood exactly what I just read. So, Jesus came to heal the brokenhearted and set captives free? He came to give sight to the blind—the spiritually blind? This is undeniably, exactly what I experienced with Him. A healed heart and being set free go hand-in-hand. The healing of a broken heart begins when you replace lies with the truth. The truth renews your mind and you are set free from the prison of your own false thoughts. Blinders come off and you see the world clearly. Only the Messiah was chosen to offer this kind of freedom, because God cares about those in bondage!

It is clear that Isaiah prophesied about the coming of Jesus in Isaiah 61. However, the fifty-third chapter of Isaiah is the most powerful chapter about the Messiah, in my opinion. In Isaiah 53, there is no question about who the chapter was written.

Who has believed our report?
And to whom has the arm of the LORD been revealed?
For He shall grow up before Him as a tender plant,
And as a root out of dry ground.
He has no form or comeliness;
And when we see Him,
There is no beauty that we should desire Him.
He is despised and rejected by men,
A Man of sorrows and acquainted with grief.
And we hid, as it were, our faces from Him;
He was despised, and we did not esteem Him.
Surely He has borne our griefs

And carried our sorrows;
Yet we esteemed Him stricken,
Smitten by God, and afflicted.
But He was wounded for our transgressions,
He was bruised for our iniquities;
The chastisement for our peace was upon Him,
And by His stripes we are healed.
All we like sheep have gone astray;
We have turned, every one, to his own way;
And the LORD has laid on Him the iniquity of us all.
He was oppressed and He was afflicted,
Yet He opened not His mouth;
He was led as a lamb to the slaughter,
And as a sheep before its shearers is silent,
So He opened not His mouth.
He was taken from prison and from judgment,
And who will declare His generation?
For He was cut off from the land of the living;
For the transgressions of My people He was stricken.
And they made His grave with the wicked—
But with the rich at His death,
Because He had done no violence,
Nor was any deceit in His mouth.
Yet it pleased the LORD to bruise Him;
He has put Him to grief.
When You make His soul an offering for sin,
He shall see His seed, He shall prolong His days,
And the pleasure of the LORD shall prosper in His hand.
[11] He shall see the labor of His soul, and be satisfied.
By His knowledge My righteous Servant shall justify many,
For He shall bear their iniquities.
Therefore I will divide Him a portion with the great,
And He shall divide the spoil with the strong,

Because He poured out His soul unto death,
And He was numbered with the transgressors,
And He bore the sin of many,
And made intercession for the transgressors. (Isaiah 53)

This sounds a lot like the guy I read about in the second part of the Bible—Jesus, the guy that was despised and rejected by others. He was a man of suffering and was wounded for our transgressions. Because of His wounds, we are healed. This Jesus guy took on what looked like some big, final atonement for the sins of the world. He Himself said in Matthew 9:12-13 that He didn't come for the righteous, but for sinners. He came to make us clean with his perfect blood that was shed for us. He also came to be a Healer and Deliverer. That is how I know Him—my Healer and Deliverer. How can I deny that He is who He says He is? I cannot. How could Isaiah have prophesied so accurately the life of Jesus so many years before He walked on earth, and it not be about Him?

When I experienced this Healer, a renewal of the mind instantly took place. I began to see the world differently. I thought differently. I had a new life in the Messiah. Romans 12:2 says, "And do not be conformed to this world, but be transformed by the renewing of your mind, that you may prove what is that good and acceptable and perfect will of God." There is an absolute transformation that takes place when you experience a renewal of the mind that can only come from Messiah.

When Kathy prayed with me for healing, I told you she said something to me that resonated deep within my spirit and I didn't even feel like it was her talking to me. The words that came from her mouth were *familiar* to my spirit. At the time, I didn't understand how her words connected to God, but I knew something happened and it was real.

By this point, you might not be surprised that I found a scripture that confirms the change in my heart. One of the first people I read about that spoke for God was Moses. In Exodus 4:12, God said to Moses, *"Now therefore, go, and I will be with your mouth and teach you what you shall say."* Moses was a prophet. A prophet is someone who hears from God and speaks for Him. This still happens today. Jesus said that when He left this world, He would send the Holy Spirit. In the book of Acts, the words of the prophet Joel were fulfilled.

"And it shall come to pass in the last days," says God, "That I will pour out of My Spirit on all flesh; Your sons and your daughters shall prophesy, Your young men shall see visions, Your old men shall dream dreams. And on My menservants and on My maidservants I will pour out My Spirit in those days; And they shall prophesy." (Acts 2:17-18)

Prophecy and prophets are all real. You can read about fulfilled prophecies in the Bible that have happened. Some are happening *right now* in this world. Just look at Israel. Do you want to know if our God is the one true God? Just read Ezekiel 36 and take a good look at Israel. God promised His people would return to the land, the waste places would be rebuilt, the land would flourish, and the people would multiply. This has been happening before our very eyes since 1948. God also said that He is not going to restore and bless Israel because they deserve it. He said He is doing it for His own Holy name! He is doing it to prove that He is God! God is simply undeniable. God gives us prophecy—another proof that He is real.

Shall I go on with more proof that the Bible is the Word of God? How can I experience so many things and later read about it in the Bible, if the Bible were not true? God is all about displaying His greatness and proving His love, if we would just pay attention and seek a relationship with Him through His Word.

As you read in Chapter 15, I was walking in the wake of a miracle. I had a renewed mind and was filled with the Spirit of Truth—the Spirit of God in my heart. However, we live in a world with a real enemy that wants to take away what God has given us. If the enemy has come after you once, he'll come after you again. The enemy comes to steal, kill, and destroy life—physical and spiritual—that was given to you by the living God.

When you experience fear, how do you feel afterwards? Drained? When you experience anxiety, do you have any energy left? When you are sad and depressed, do you feel full of energy or low on fuel? What are these feelings? They are negative emotions that come from the root of *fear*. Fear is from the enemy, so when he can get you to live and operate in fear (anxiety, depression, anger, or hate), your life diminishes. And when your life diminishes, you walk in darkness and are slowly destroyed in the spiritual realm. This is what Jesus was talking about in John 10:10 when He said, "The thief does not come except to steal, and to kill, and to destroy. I have come that they may have life, and that they may have it more abundantly."

In the temple on the last day of the Feast of Booths, Jesus also said,

> On the last day, that great day of the feast, Jesus stood and cried out, saying, "If anyone thirsts, let him come to Me and drink. He who believes in Me, as the Scripture has said, out of his heart will flow rivers of living water. (John 7:37-38)

He is saying that He will quench our spiritual thirst and give us life in our spirits. He is the One who gives life!

The enemy came to steal my life again through drug addiction. Yes, I received a healing and I experienced a real miracle and God did wonderful things for me right before my very eyes. But the pressure and disappointment from one event led me right down a familiar path and I completely turned my back on God. How could someone that experienced the things I did and turn their back on God? To my surprise, I read about a group of people who constantly did the same thing to God—His chosen people, the Israelites.

God took His people out of slavery in Egypt, parted the Red Sea for them to cross on a dry seabed, supernaturally guided them in the desert, continually appeared to them, and made manna fall from the sky for them to eat. He made Himself so real and so undeniable to these people and they still turned their backs on God when things got tough. Oh, how I connected with these people when I read about them. God called them a "stiff-necked people" and I admit, so am I!

It didn't stop there. All throughout the Bible are stories of God and the people who turn their backs on Him. Thank goodness His love for them was everlasting. We are no different from the people in these stories, in that we separate ourselves from Him when we sin. Fortunately, God never changes, and had a plan for our sin.

> For God so loved the world that He gave His only begotten
> Son, that whoever believes in Him should not perish but
> have everlasting life. (John 3:16)

He sent a final sacrifice, a final atonement for the world, because He loved this world and everyone in it. The power of the shed blood of the Messiah is available to everyone that believes in Him. When we accept this truth, we are in a perfect relationship with our Heavenly Father.

When I got arrested for the last time, I had been on the longest, deepest and darkest drug binge of my life. I was as low as one could get. It doesn't get much lower than a jail cell, unless you are six feet under the ground with no more chances. I sat in that low spot in my jail cell, and a new side of Jesus was revealed to me. I had known Him as the Healer of my heart and the true Son of God. I absolutely believed that He was divine. But, when I sat in my jail cell and agreed in my spirit that "I messed up" towards Him, something happened. I knew that my life would never truly be where it needed to be...if I didn't do my part.

You see, God had already done His part by sending His Son as atonement for our sins. We can receive answered prayers and miracles all day long, and *still* choose to do the wrong thing since we have a free will. If we truly want to walk in freedom, walk in our healings, walk in our miracles, and our answered prayers, we have to do our part by *choosing* life. God told His people in the desert in Deuteronomy 30:19:

> I call heaven and earth as witnesses today against you, that
> I have set before you life and death, blessing and cursing;
> therefore choose life, that both you and your descendants
> may live.

Choose life! It is a *choice*!

There is a Jewish holiday with great spiritual significance to me called, Tu'B'Shvat. I heard an explanation of it one day that really spoke to my spirit. It is a holiday observed in the dead of winter, celebrating the new year of the trees. That seems confusing, doesn't it? Why would the new year of the trees be celebrated when the trees are not green and full of flowers and fruit? Why would this be celebrated in the dead of winter during the darkest, coldest days? Because this is where life starts, beloved.

For the trees, it is during this time—in the dead of winter—that the sap comes from the deepest part of the tree, up through the trunk. A *process* begins and you will not see the fruit of that process for months and months. So it is with us. Our process begins with a *choice*—a choice to *choose life* as the Father commanded. When we make this choice to change our lives, do better, turn away from sin, and turn to the One who gives life, a *process* begins in the deepest part of our being. You may not see the fruit of that process, that decision you made, for many months. However, it will come.

When I sat in that jail cell on February 7, 2007, I made a decision. I chose life. I said to God, "Ok. I'm done." And I know that in that very moment, I was delivered from drug addiction. You might wonder, was it the decision I made to stop using drugs, or was I actually delivered from drug use? I believe there has to be a desire from the deepest part of your being to be set free from something. I *chose* to be done using drugs. However, I think when we "choose life," when we choose to do the right thing, we are allowing God to be involved. I do not doubt for one minute

God's involvement in me being drug-free. I've never thought about using another drug again and never felt the temptation to use again. I know in that moment, when I made that choice, I was done and I was going to do whatever it took to have my life back. I know I was delivered by the power of Jesus!

As with the trees, when that process started from the deepest part within me, I did not see the fruit of that choice for a long time. I was in the dead of winter and in the middle of dark days. I had work to do and sometimes, it was hard to keep going—but I had everything I needed to make it. I had the Spirit of the Living God inside me and His living Word—the Messiah—directing my steps. He was my life-giver, the living water inside me that helped me keep going. He said in John 14:6, "I am the way, the truth, and the life. No one comes to the Father except through me."

At the Western Wall watching men gather, sing and dance together on Jerusalem Day.

Standing in the midst of God's fulfilled promise of restoring HIS people to THEIR land!

CHAPTER 19

Undeniable God

Dear brothers and sisters…

Is this just a story full of coincidences? Or, is there something more to it? Does it seem like there was a design, a plan, with supernatural intervention? Were there times in my life that seemed like there was supernatural protection around me? Or was the pizza driver that brought two 12-year-olds to safety late at night a coincidence? How did I get to a safe place in the middle of the night when I blacked out from heavy drug use? Does this seem like something that can be explained?

How did I know there was a God from a young age without any teaching or training? Are we created with that understanding in our spirits? How did I know, sitting in Catholic Church, that I could pray to God Himself and confess my sins without the help of another human? How did I know that prayers said to Mary or saints were not reaching God? Where did these hunches come from? How did I know God heard me when I prayed? What made me toss everything out that was taught in my Catholic upbringing, except Jesus? The still, small voice of an undeniable God did.

How did I start having dreams about things that would happen the next day, days later, weeks later, or even a month later? Who was showing me these things? How did I know things about people that I couldn't have possibly known, or see a future event before it happened?

Who showed me these things? An undeniable God did.

Who told a man I didn't even know to give me his car when I needed one the most? Was it a coincidence that God told me to contact him eight years later when this man needed a testimony to share with his church? Is that a coincidence? Of course not! This is God stuff!

I am a walking miracle. I should have died while strung out on drugs, many times. I was delivered from prison sentences when everyone, in the natural, told me to prepare for prison. Where did that glimmer of hope come from that caused me to pray and fast for nine months? It came from God, who never left me! It was not because I am good, but because He is good and these interventions glorified Him in the end. I deserved prison, but God would rather be glorified. I received miraculous healings of the heart, with supernatural downloads of truth into my spirit, which cannot be denied. They are rock-solid truths that changed my life. I have heard the voice of God!

How did I experience things in my life and later read about it in the Bible? Is that a coincidence? This is the evidence of an undeniable God. He makes Himself known in so many ways—we just have to pay attention.

I want to reiterate that I did not write this book because I thought it was a good idea or because I thought I was special in some way. I kept feeling the pressing of God to write but didn't lift a finger until I received the exact confirmation I prayed for. This book was not written because it is about me. This book was written because it is about God, and these testimonies are about Him.

The "me" part of my life is over. I searched for answers in life in all the wrong places. By the grace of God, I found the answer I was looking for. The answer to life is God.

1 John 4:8 says, "He who does not love does not know God, for God is love." God is love. I lived many years of my life believing that I was not worthy of love. The enemy had me believing that I was not worthy of the very reason I was created. This will destroy anyone. I lived in a constant battle but I won with the power of the Truth. I now live my

life immersed in the love of God's Son, the living Word, the Messiah, because my life is His. Being a follower of Him does not mean that life is going to be perfect or you are not going to have troubles. Jesus said in John 16:33,

> These things I have spoken to you, that in Me you may have peace. In the world you will have tribulation; but be of good cheer, I have overcome the world.

Nobody can escape trouble. But what it does mean is you will know *Who* to walk through this life *with*, in the midst of your troubles.

God desires a relationship with everyone on earth. It doesn't matter what you've done, what your religious upbringing was, or if you struggle with the thought of there not even being a God. He wants a relationship with you. He wants to walk with you through this life. There is no need that He can't meet. If you have a broken heart, He is the healer of the heart. If you are in chains, he is a chain breaker. If you are sick, He has the power to heal. If you need a renewal of the mind, He is here to renew it. If you are addicted to something, He is here to deliver you. If you are stuck or lost, He will make a way for you. Are you sorry and ashamed for something in the past? Ask the Lord to forgive you. He is full of grace! Are you lost in sin? He is here to save you. Are you looking for love? He *is* love! He is the Savior of the world whose blood was shed as the final atonement for sin and that blood sacrifice will wash you white as snow.

If you don't know Him, He is waiting for you, knocking on the door of your heart. He is waiting for you to invite Him in. He is a personal God and loves you more than you could ever imagine. He is the answer to everything in this life. He is undeniable. I am living proof.

So, who is God? The very first verses we read in the Bible are Genesis 1:1-5:

> In the beginning God created the heavens and the earth. The

earth was without form, and void; and darkness was on the face of the deep. And the Spirit of God was hovering over the face of the waters. Then God said, "Let there be light"; and there was light. And God saw the light, that it was good; and God divided the light from the darkness. God called the light Day, and the darkness He called Night. So the evening and the morning were the first day.

Right here, in the first few verses of the *Holy Bible*, we see God created the universe when He *spoke*. God *spoke*, and it was done.

In the beginning was the Word, and the Word was with God, and the Word was God. He was in the beginning with God. All things were made through Him, and without Him nothing was made that was made. In Him was life, and the life was the light of men. (John 1:1-4)

This is Jesus, the Messiah. He is the powerful, living Word of God.

God promised to send someone to save His people, and He did. He sent His son, Jesus, to die on the cross, saving us from a spiritual death, giving us eternal life when we leave this planet. When Jesus left, He sent His Holy Spirit to dwell on this Earth, in the hearts of all believers.

Jesus is exactly who He said He is. He is the Word of God in the flesh, holy and divine, and the Messiah of the world. He was the final atonement for the sins of the world and a precious gift, available to all of us. He is the answer to everything in life. He is the way, the truth, and the life, and nobody comes to the Father except through Him. He is the light of the world. He is the One that has brought me to where I am today. I have experienced Him. I know Him. I know He is real. He is undeniable. I can go straight to the throne room of God the Father because of Him. His blood washes away every despicable thing I ever did. Through Him, I am in perfect relationship with the Father and nothing can take that away. He was the answer to *everything* I was ever looking for in this life.

My life is no longer about me. It is about Him. My life story, this book, has nothing to do with what I have accomplished or how far I have come. It is about *Him.* It is my job, as His child and someone with a testimony, to share what God has done for me and how I came to my undeniable faith in Him. There will come a time when we all will reach the end of our life. One day, we will all face God. When I leave this life and pass on to the next, all I want is my God to look me in my eyes and say, "Well done, good and faithful servant."

I pray you find everything you are looking for in this life in the *Undeniable God.*

Grace and shalom to you in the Messiah Yeshua (Jesus),

Katherine

Order online at:

- CertaPublishing.com/UndeniableGod
- Phone: 855-77-CERTA
- Email: Info@CertaPublishing.com

Also available through Amazon.com